INTERCOM 2000

Anna Uhl Chamot

Isobel Rainey de Diaz

Joan Baker de Gonzalez

Richard Yorkey

Heinle & Heinle Publishers
A Division of Wadsworth, Inc.
Boston, Massachusetts 02116

Publisher: Stanley J. Galek
Editorial Director: Christopher Foley
Project Editor: Anita L. Raducanu
Content Editor: Margot Gramer
Assistant Editors: Erik Gundersen
Nancy A. Mann

Production Supervisor: Patricia Jalbert
Production Manager: Erek Smith
Designed and Produced by: Publishers' Graphics Inc.
Prepress Color and Integration:
FinalCopy Electronic Publishing Services
Cover: The Graphics Studio/Gerry Rosentswieg

Acknowledgments

The authors and publisher would like to acknowledge the contributions of the following individuals who reviewed the *Intercom 2000* program at various stages of development and who offered many helpful insights and suggestions:

- Mary J. Erickson and Galen Shaney, *English Language Institute, University of Texas, Pan American*
- Toni Sachs Hadi, *New York City Board of Education*
- Katy Cox, *Casa Thomas Jefferson, Brasília, Brazil*
- Ronald A. Reese, *Long Beach (CA) Unified School District*
- Ruthann Hilferty, *Paterson (NJ) Board of Education*
- Lúcia de Aragão, Sonia Godoy, and Rosa Erlichman, *União Cultural, São Paulo, Brazil*
- Peggy Kazkaz, *William Rainey Harper College*
- Roland G. Axelson, Diane Hazel, and Mary Wayne Pierce, *Hartford (CT) Public Schools*
- Keith A. Buchanan, *Fairfax County (VA) Public Schools*

Heinle & Heinle Publishers is a division of
Wadsworth, Inc.

Manufactured in the United States of America.

ISBN 0-8384-1813-9

10   9   8   7   6   5   4

Contents

COMMUNICATION	GRAMMAR	SKILLS

COMMUNICATION	GRAMMAR	SKILLS

COMMUNICATION	GRAMMAR	SKILLS

PHOTO CREDITS

TEXT/REALIA CREDITS

Intercom 2000

The People

Tom Logan

MARITAL STATUS: married; 3 children

OCCUPATION: travel agent (Wells Travel Agency)

PASTIMES: working in the yard, listening to music

Adela Logan

MARITAL STATUS: married; 3 children

OCCUPATION: student and homemaker

SCHOOL: Winfield Technical Institute

MAJOR: computer programming

PASTIMES: listening to music, going to the movies, sewing

Sam Logan

AGE: 20 years old

MARITAL STATUS: single

OCCUPATION: mechanic (Winfield Garage) and student

SCHOOL: Winfield Community College

MAJOR: engineering

SPORTS: running, swimming, soccer

Bob Logan

AGE: 17 years old

SCHOOL: Winfield High School

SPORTS: basketball, soccer, tennis

PASTIME: playing chess

BEST FRIEND: Mike Young

Lisa Logan

AGE: 12 years old

SCHOOL: Winfield Elementary School

ABILITIES: sings well

SPORTS: ice skating

PASTIME: sewing, playing chess

BEST FRIEND: Joyce Young

Elinor Young

MARITAL STATUS: married; 4 children

OCCUPATION: doctor (Winfield Hospital)

PASTIMES: playing tennis, going for long walks, going to museums

Howard Young

MARITAL STATUS: married; 4 children

OCCUPATION: engineer

PASTIMES: playing tennis, swimming

Liz Young

AGE: 21 years old

MARITAL STATUS: single

OCCUPATION: international telephone operator

LANGUAGES: German, French, Spanish

Mike Young

AGE: 17 years old

SCHOOL: Winfield High School

SPORTS: soccer, basketball, tennis

PASTIMES: dancing

BEST FRIEND: Bob Logan

Ted Young

AGE: 15 years old

SCHOOL: Winfield High School

SPORTS: soccer, swimming

PASTIME: playing chess

Joyce Young

AGE: 12 years old

SCHOOL: Winfield Elementary School

ABILITIES: draws well

SPORTS: soccer, basketball, tennis

PASTIME: dancing

BEST FRIEND: Lisa Logan

Pablo Nava

MARITAL STATUS:
married; 2 children

OCCUPATION:
architect

ADDRESS:
Calle Paloma, 5
Mexico, D.F.,
Mexico

Melanie Nava

MARITAL STATUS:
married; 2 children

PLACE OF BIRTH: Los
Angeles, California

OCCUPATION: English
teacher

PASTIMES: travel,
photography

Carlos Nava

AGE: 18 years old

PLACE OF BIRTH:
Mexico, D.F.,
Mexico

OCCUPATION: student
(last year of high
school)

LANGUAGES: Spanish
and English

Ana Nava

AGE: 14 years old

PLACE OF BIRTH:
Mexico, D.F.,
Mexico

OCCUPATION: student

LANGUAGES: Spanish
and English

Maria Gomez de Nava

MARITAL STATUS:
widowed; 1 child
(Pablo Nava)

ADDRESS:
Calle Paloma, 5
Mexico, D.F.,
Mexico

Gino Leone

PLACE OF BIRTH:
Naples, Italy

OCCUPATION: cook
(Roma Restaurant)
and cooking teacher
(Winfield
Community College)

SPORTS: swimming

PASTIMES: reading,
painting

ENGAGED TO: Cristina
Silva

Cristina Silva

PLACE OF BIRTH:
Bogota, Colombia

OCCUPATION: cashier
(Roma Restaurant)
and student

SCHOOL: Winfield
Community College

MAJOR: art history

PASTIMES: dancing,
playing chess

ENGAGED TO: Gino
Leone

Gloria Rivera

AGE: 16 years old

SCHOOL: Winfield
High School

PLACE OF BIRTH: New
York City

SPORTS: volleyball,
tennis

ABILITIES: plays the
guitar well, sings

LANGUAGE: Spanish

Toshio Ito

PLACE OF BIRTH:
Kyoto, Japan

OCCUPATION: flight
attendant (World
Airlines)

LIKES: travel,
working with people

SPORTS: swimming,
running

Nhu Trinh

PLACE OF BIRTH:
Saigon (currently
Ho Chi Minh City),
Vietnam

OCCUPATION: flight
attendant (World
Airlines)

PASTIME: going to
the movies

Sekila Manzikala

PLACE OF BIRTH:
Kinshasa, Zaire

OCCUPATION: student

SCHOOL: Winfield
Community College

ABILITIES: sings well

LANGUAGES: French,
Lingala, English

COMMUNICATION
Talking about the news ▪ Talking about family life

GRAMMAR
Questions with *why* and reasons with *to* + verb ▪ Result clauses with *so*

SKILLS
Reading, listening to, and writing short news stories ▪ Writing a short report and presenting it orally

What's in the News?

Here are some articles from the Winfield Daily News.

❖ Engaged to be married ❖

Mr. and Mrs. Eduardo Silva of Bogota, Colombia, are happy to announce the engagement of their daughter Cristina Ana Silva to Gino Antonio Leone. Miss Silva is studying art history at Winfield Community College and Mr. Leone is the chef at the Roma Restaurant. The wedding will take place at St. Mark's Church in Winfield on October 5th. The reception will be at the Roma.

Benjamins have a daughter

Mr. and Mrs. Leon Benjamin are proud to announce the birth of their first child, Andrea Jean. She was born at Winfield Hospital on June 9 at 11:10 PM.

Black History Month

Winfield Public Library is pleased to announce a special program to celebrate Black History Month. The well-known actor Albert Eaton will perform a one-man show entitled "MLK: His Life and Times."

UPI/BETTMANN

In the show, Eaton recreates the life and times of the late civil rights leader Martin Luther King, Jr., through music and drama. Performances are at 3:30 and 7:30, Thursday through Saturday. Admission free. Telephone: 536-5400.

SPORTS
High School _____

Parents Beat Students

The parents' soccer team beat the students 4-2 in a wild and exciting match yesterday at Winfield Stadium. It was the first win for the parents since the annual event started five years ago. Adela Logan led the parents to victory with three goals. Her son, Bob Logan, scored the only two goals for the losing team. It was both a happy and a sad day for the Logan family!

College _____

Winfield Community College Senior Wins State Tournament

Ginny Lewis took the title away from defending state tennis champion, Susan Murray, yesterday in three straight sets, 6-1, 6-3, 6-4. This was the first time a Winfield student has played in the state finals. Ginny brought home a trophy and a $1000 scholarship.

1 Presentation

Questions with *why* and reasons with *to* + verb

A

A: **Why** did the Benjamins put an
announcement in the paper?
B: **To announce** the birth of their daughter
Andrea Jean.

B

A: **Why** did Cristina call Liz?
B: **To tell** her about her engagement.

2 Practice

**Ask and answer *why* questions. Use the information in the newspaper articles on
page 6 for 1-5. Make up your own answers for 6-10.**

> A: Why did Gino call Cristina?
> B: To talk about their wedding.

1. Why did Cristina's parents put an announcement in the newspaper?
2. Why is the Winfield Public Library planning a special program?
3. Why did the Youngs and the Logans go to the library on Thursday
   night?
4. Why did the Benjamins put an announcement in the newspaper?
5. Why did Adela Logan go to Winfield Stadium yesterday?

Now make up your own answers.

6. Why did Cristina write to her aunt?
7. Why did Mr. and Mrs. Silva write to the Winfield Daily News?
8. Why did the Logans go to Winfield Stadium yesterday?
9. Why did Ginny Lewis play tennis in the State Tournament?
10. Why did you come to class today?

3 Vocabulary in Context

Talking about the news

> Some verbs have a noun form. For example; *compete* is a verb and *competition* is a noun.

Verb	Noun
announce	announcement
arrive	arrival
be born	birth
celebrate	celebration
get engaged	engagement
get married	marriage
receive	reception
score	score
wed	wedding
win	win

Use the information from the newspaper articles on page 6. Complete each sentence with the correct form of one of the verbs or nouns above.

1. Gino and Cristina just _____ their _____ .
   They _____ this month. Cristina _____ a beautiful ring from Gino, and they _____ their engagement with a special dinner. Cristina and Gino are going to _____ on October 5th. They want to have a large _____ at St. Mark's Church, and a small _____ for their friends and family at the Roma. They want to have a long and happy _____ .

2. The _____ for Black History Month at the Winfield Public Library is going to have a special one-man show. You need to _____ early to get a good seat.

3. Mr. and Mrs. Leon Benjamin announced the _____ of their daughter. They put an _____ in the newspaper. Andrea Jean _____ on June 9. The Benjamins are very happy about the _____ of their first child.

4. Ginny Lewis _____ the state tennis championship. It was the first _____ for a Winfield student.

5. Bob Logan _____ the two goals for the students' team. The final _____ was 4-2.

4 Interaction

Look at your local newspaper, or the newspaper articles on page 6, and talk about the news. Use the vocabulary in *3*. Ask questions using *who, what, where, when*. Here is a model.

> A: Here's an article about a wedding.
> B: Oh? Who got married?
> A: Kim Penh and Kan Sokhom.
> B: When was the wedding?
> A: Saturday, March 27th.

5 Reentry

Yes/no questions and answers

Ask and answer questions about the newspaper articles on page 6. Be sure to use the correct verb tense.

> Ginny Lewis / win / tennis championship / last year
> A: Did Ginny Lewis win the tennis championship last year?
> B: No, she won it this year.

1. Bob Logan / score / three goals / yesterday
2. Benjamins / have / new son
3. Andrea Jean Benjamin / be born / at Winfield Hospital
4. Cristina and Gino / announce / their engagement
5. Cristina / be born / in New York
6. Gino and Cristina / get engaged / in Bogota
7. Albert Eaton / sing / in his show / at the Winfield Public Library
8. Bob Logan / feel / happy / after the soccer game
9. Mr. and Mrs. Lewis / feel / proud / their daughter Ginny
10. Cristina / go / be / nervous / at the wedding

6 Presentation

Result clauses with *so*

The result of the action or situation in the first clause is given in a second clause that starts with **so**.

The Logans are usually a happy family, but sometimes they have problems. They live in a small apartment, **so** they don't have a lot of room for their things. There are too many things and there is too much noise in their apartment! They would like to move into a house, **so** this year they're all working very hard.

Tom Logan needs to make more money, **so** he works on weekends. Adela wants to get a job, too, **so** she's studying computer programming. Bob and Sam are students, **so** they work when they're not at school. Lisa is only twelve, **so** she can't work. Her parents ask her to do some chores around the house to help the family. But Lisa is lazy sometimes, **so** she "forgets" to do her chores.

Maybe when the Logans have a new house, they can all relax more.

7 Practice

Expand each sentence by adding a *so*-clause that tells the result. You may choose phrases from the box or make up your own.

> **Useful Phrases**
>
> | | |
> |---|---|
> | cook at home | study at night |
> | study hard | work on weekends |
> | drive his old one | clean the house and make a cake |
> | get a job | get up early |
> | go to bed early tonight | work and save money |

> Cristina and Gino want to go to Paris on their honeymoon, so they have to work and save money.

1. Adela needs money.

2. Bob has a difficult exam.

3. Sam works during the day.

4. Lisa has to clean her room.

5. Tom can't buy a new car.

6. Tom has to go to work early tomorrow.

7. The Logans can't eat at restaurants very often.

8. Bob goes to school during the week.

9. Lisa wants to invite some friends to her house for a party.

10. The Logans want to move into a house.

8 Interaction

Complete the first column of the chart with real or imaginary information. Then talk with a classmate. Ask and answer questions about how you each felt last night, last Saturday, and last vacation. Tell what you did, using a *so*-clause. As you talk, complete the information about how your classmate felt.

> A: What did you do last night, _____ ?
> B: Oh, I was tired, so I went to bed early.

When	How I Felt	How My Classmate Felt
Last night		
Last Saturday		
Last vacation		

Talking about family life

Life in the United States

In the United States, when a man and woman decide to get married, they usually announce their engagement to their families and friends. Their families often send an announcement to a newspaper. Many years ago, a lot of people were engaged for several years, but nowadays engagements are usually short.

Usually both families participate in the wedding. The **mother-in-law** and **father-in-law** of the **bride** often invite both families to a dinner the evening before the wedding. The bride's parents usually pay for their daughter's wedding and reception. At the reception after the wedding, the guests eat, drink, dance, and talk. After this celebration, the bride and **groom** often take a trip. This trip is called a **honeymoon.**

When children are born, the parents sometimes announce each birth in the newspaper and send cards to their friends. Many years ago, most people had a lot of children, but today families are usually smaller. When people are very unhappy with their marriage, they can get a **divorce**.

When people get older, they think about **retirement.** In the United States, many people **retire** from work when they are sixty-five, but some people continue to work after that age. Retired people have a lot of free time, so they can try new sports or hobbies, take courses, or travel. For some husbands and wives, retirement is a second honeymoon!

10 Practice

Complete the paragraph with the correct form of one of the words in *3* or *9*.

My father-in-law, Stanley Peterson, who is sixty-five, (1) _____ from his job last week. He and his family were invited to a (2) _____ given by his company. I didn't really want to go, but my husband, Dan, said, "We should help my father celebrate his (3) _____." So we went, and I had to listen to my (4) _____ tell his whole life story — again!

Stanley Peterson said that he and his wife were (5) _____ for seven years before they got (6) _____ because he couldn't find a job. He said that no one came to their (7) _____ because he didn't have any friends. He said that they returned from their (8) _____ after only one day because he got sick. He said that when their son (my husband Dan) was (9) _____, he gave the newspaper the wrong spelling of the baby's name, so the newspaper announced that the Petersons had a daughter — Danielle!

I looked at my (10) _____, and she smiled. "I almost got a (11) _____ when I saw that newspaper (12) _____," she said.

11 Listening

First Listening

Number your paper from 1-10. Listen to the news announcement, and write *T* (true), *F* (false), or *NG* (not given).

1. Ms. Isabelle Saunders is an actress.
2. This is Ms. Saunders' first marriage.
3. Ms. Saunders married a TV actor today.
4. Mr. Russell Barlak is president of a company.
5. This is Mr. Barlak's second marriage.
6. Ms. Saunders is happy about her new marriage.
7. The new husband and wife are going on a honeymoon.
8. Mr. Barlak makes a lot of money.
9. Ms. Saunders made four movies last year.
10. Mr. Barlak's computers are easy to use.

Now number your paper from 1-4. Listen to the news announcement a second time. Then decide whether you agree or disagree with the statements below. Write *Agree* or *Disagree*. Then work with a classmate and tell why you agree or disagree.

1. Isabelle Saunders is probably very talented.

2. Russell Barlak is probably very rich.

3. Ms. Saunders and Mr. Barlak will probably be very happy.

4. Ms. Saunders does not like to work all the time.

12 Reading

Before You Read

1. Do you read the advice column in the newspaper?

2. Do you write to a newspaper to ask for advice?

3. What advice could you ask for?

4. Do people need advice on good manners?
   Why or why not?

First Reading

Read the questions below before reading the "Dear Mrs. Gently" advice column. Think about the questions as you read. After reading, write answers to the questions. Discuss your answers in small groups.

1. Why is "Puzzled in Peoria" not happy with the invitation?

2. What is her husband's point of view?

3. Does Mrs. Gently agree with "Puzzled in Peoria" or with her husband? Why?

4. What is a "potluck dinner?"

5. What advice does Mrs. Gently give?

Mrs. Gently

Dear Mrs. Gently,

    A friend of mine is giving a big party at her home to celebrate her wedding anniversary. My husband and I received an invitation that included this note at the bottom:

    "In order to help pay for the food and drinks, you are asked to make a contribution of $10.00 at the door."

    Don't you think this is incredibly rude? I think we should refuse the invitation, but my husband says we should go to the party and pay the $10.00. He tells me that Jim (my friend's husband) is out of a job at the moment, so they are really short of money.

    What do you think?

Puzzled in Peoria

Dear Puzzled,

    In all my many years of dispensing advice on matters of taste and manners, I have never heard of such a preposterous solution to financial embarrassment. Does your friend think that she's operating a restaurant? The lack of money does not excuse such rudeness. If your friend wants contributions from guests, she should plan an informal potluck dinner. It's perfectly acceptable to ask guests to bring a main dish or salad or dessert to a party. It is truly tasteless to ask for a contribution of money.

    My advice is simple. You should politely but firmly decline this "invitation."

Mrs. Gently

Second Reading

A. Sit in a small group and read the "Dear Mrs. Gently" column again. Then discuss the meanings of the words and phrases below. Decide on a definition or a different way to say the same thing. Share your work with other groups.

Word or Phrase	My Group's Definition
1. wedding anniversary	
2. contribution	
3. incredibly rude	
4. refuse	
5. out of a job	
6. short of money	
7. to dispense advice	
8. preposterous	
9. financial	
10. to decline	

B. Write a few sentences telling why you agree or disagree with Mrs. Gently's advice. You can give personal reasons, or you can talk about what is or isn't good manners in your country. Share your sentences with the class.

13 Writing and Speaking

A. Write notes for a short oral report about "The Perfect Wedding." You can talk about a wedding you went to, or an imaginary wedding. Use these guidelines:

Describe the "perfect" wedding. Tell who gets married, where they get married, who is at the wedding, what the wedding is like, what kind of celebration there is, what people eat and drink, what gifts people give, and other things that make this wedding "perfect."

B. Practice your talk with a partner. Write five questions about the information in your talk.

C. Sit with three or four classmates. Take turns giving your talks about "The Perfect Wedding." After your talk, ask your five questions to see if your classmates remember what you said.

14 Final Activity

Pretend you are a reporter for a newspaper. You need to write a short article. Choose either an article about an engagement or an article about a sports game that your town's team won. Role play a telephone conversation with a classmate. In the conversation, find out either the information you need from the parent of the woman who is engaged, or find out the information you need from the coach of the winning team. Ask questions using *Who? What? Where? When? How? Why?* Then write the story and share it with the class.

> A: Good morning, Mr./Mrs. _____ . My name is
> _____ . I'm a reporter for the Winfield Daily News.
> I'm writing an article about Winfield people in the news — such
> as your daughter. Could you tell me about your daughter's
> engagement?
> B: Of course, I'll be glad to answer your questions.
> A: Thank you. First, who is your daughter engaged to?
> B: His name is _____ .
> A: What does he do?
> B: He's a _____ . etc.

UNIT 2

COMMUNICATION
Reading and talking about newspaper articles, ads, and announcements ▪ Making and responding to suggestions ▪ Talking about time and TV schedules

GRAMMAR
Telling time with *past, after, to,* and *of* ▪ Questions with *How long . . . ?* ▪ *Learn to* + verb ▪ Past of *become*

SKILLS
Writing a classified ad ▪ Reading about special events in a newspaper

Another Look at the News

Newspapers contain many types of articles and ads. Here are some examples.

Chinese Artist in Winfield

The Winfield Art Museum is pleased to announce the acquisition of a new sculpture by Chang Ling. Mr. Chang Ling, a famous Chinese artist, donated one of his sculptures to the museum. In honor of Ling's generous donation, there will be a public reception for the artist on June 10th. During the reception, guests can view the spectacular sculpture.

Last night, the director of the Winfield Art Museum, Mr. Arthur Stevenson, hosted a private reception for Mr. Chang Ling at his home. At the reception, Mr. Stevenson thanked his honored guest for his gift to the museum. Mr. Stevenson hopes that the museum will acquire more treasures like Mr. Ling's sculpture in the future.

Toyota *TYSON'S CORNER*

New 1991 Toyota
$10,500

Ready for immediate delivery!
Inexpensive — don't wait!

THE ROMA RESTAURANT

2205 Prince Street
656-8700

• *delicious Italian food*
• *reasonable prices*
• *private dining rooms*
• *open 11 AM to 11 PM*

★★★*"Great food at great prices . . . Try Gino's Roma spaghetti sauce!"*
— Mame Harrison, Gourmet News

The Best Apartment Value in Washington in an Unbeatable Location!
1500 Massachusetts Avenue
SPECIAL!

STUDIO $395/month   1 BEDROOM $518/month

ALL UTILITIES INCLUDED
These apartments offer incomparable downtown convenience. Only 3 blocks to Metro Station and within a few blocks of fine restaurants, shopping, and the heart of downtown. Laundry Room, 24-hour Garage Parking available. Drugstore on premises.

MANAGEMENT OFFICE OPEN 7 DAYS PER WEEK
PHONE 293-1300
Equal Housing Opportunity

REGENTS SQUARE STATION

1, 2, & 3 BR apts. with den available now with ultra-modern kitchens, carpeted halls, pvt. laundry in park-like setting w/extensive rec. facils. Huge rooms with walk-in closets. Pvt. off street park'g. Extremely well maintained. From $395. ALL UTILITIES INCLUDED. Open Mon-Fri 8:30-5; Sat. 10-2. Directions: 495 to Penn. Ave., R. Silver Hill, 5 blocks.

CALL 437-3555

Vocabulary in Context 🔲

Reading newspaper articles

Use the information from the newspaper article "Chinese Artist in Winfield" to complete the paragraph below with the correct word from the list. Use each word from the list only once.

acquire	private
director	public
donated	sculpture
exhibit	spectacular
guests	treasure

   The famous Chinese artist Chang Ling (1) _____ a beautiful new (2) _____ to the Winfield Art Museum. The (3) _____ of the museum, Mr. Arthur Stevenson, invited the artist to a (4) _____ reception at his home. Mr. Stevenson thanked Mr. Ling for the (5) _____ gift and said, "We want to (6) _____ more works of art like this for Winfield." During the reception, the (7) _____ were given the opportunity to see the museum's new (8) _____ . A (9) _____ reception on June 10 will honor this new (10) _____ at the Winfield Art Museum.

Practice

Newspaper announcements often give only essential, or very important, information. After reading the newspaper article "Chinese Artist in Winfield," complete the following announcement about the private reception:

Announcement:	
What type of event:	_____
In honor of whom:	_____
When:	_____
Where:	_____
Why:	_____

3 Vocabulary in Context

Reading newspaper ads

Find each of the following words in the ads on page 17. Then choose the best meaning for the words.

convenience	reasonable
included	studio
inexpensive	ultramodern
on the premises	unbeatable

1. A **reasonable** price means that it. . .
   a. costs a lot of money.
   b. does not cost a lot of money.

2. The Toyota is **inexpensive**.
   a. It costs a lot of money.
   b. It doesn't cost a lot of money.

3. An apartment in an **unbeatable** location is. . .
   a. in an excellent part of town.
   b. not in an excellent part of town.

4. A **studio** apartment is very. . .
   a. large.
   b. small.

5. If something is **on the premises**, it is. . .
   a. two blocks away.
   b. in the building.

6. An **ultramodern** kitchen is. . .
   a. not very new.
   b. very new.

7. If utilities (electricity, water, etc.) are **included**, it means you. . .
   a. have to pay extra for them.
   b. don't have to pay extra for them.

8. Downtown **convenience** means that the apartment is. . .
   a. close to stores and restaurants downtown.
   b. far away from stores and restaurants downtown.

4 Reentry

Negative statements

Review the articles on page 17. Write five false statements about the articles. Then work with a partner. Take turns giving a false statement, disagreeing with each other, and correcting the information.

> A: Mr. Stevenson paid a lot of money for Chang Ling's sculpture.
> B: No, he didn't. Chang Ling donated it to the museum.
>
> B: The apartment at 1500 Massachusetts Avenue is really far away from public transportation.
> A: No, it isn't. It's only three blocks to the public transportation.

5 Interaction

Look at the Restaurant Guide. Then follow the instructions below for a conversation with a classmate. After the conversation, change roles.

Restaurant Guide		
Prices	**Food**	**Service**
$$$$ very expensive	¶¶¶¶ excellent	★★★★ excellent
$$$ expensive	¶¶¶ very good	★★★ very good
$$ reasonable	¶¶ good	★★ good
$ inexpensive	¶ fair	★ fair

The Paris Café $$$$ ¶ ★★★
645 Harbor Avenue
French food in a beautiful old building.
View of the harbor.

Mario's Place $$$$ ¶¶¶¶ ★★★★
673 Broadway
Excellent seafood in a modern dining room.

Old Mexico $ ¶¶¶ ★
25 Main Street
A small, busy restaurant serving good
Mexican food.

The Roma $$ ¶¶¶ ★★★
2205 Prince Street
A friendly, relaxing restaurant with good
Italian food.

> A: Greet your friend.
> B: Return the greeting.
> A: Ask your friend if he/she is hungry.
> B: Respond that you're very hungry.
> A: Exclaim, "Great!" Suggest going to one of the restaurants above.
> B: You like the idea, but explain why you can't go. For example, you don't like that kind of food, or the restaurant's too expensive.
> A: Say, "No problem." Suggest another place to eat.
> B: Accept the offer.

6 Presentation

Telling time with *past, after, to,* and *of*

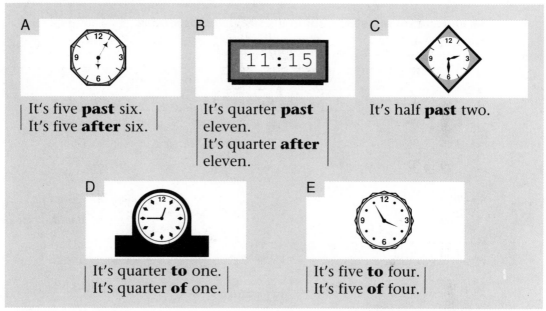

A It's five **past** six.
It's five **after** six.

B It's quarter **past** eleven.
It's quarter **after** eleven.

C It's half **past** two.

D It's quarter **to** one.
It's quarter **of** one.

E It's five **to** four.
It's five **of** four.

7 Practice

Look at the clocks below and say what time it is.

1.

2.

3.

4.

5.

6.

7.

8.

8 Reentry

Questions with *What time . . . ?*

Ask and answer questions about the television programs.

TV TODAY	Tuesday, January 10		
	Channel 4	**Channel 5**	**Channel 9**
6:00	World News	Evening News	News of the Day
6:30	World of Sports	Sports and Weather	Today's Games
7:00	Dr. Nolan	Movie: *One Long Summer*	In Town
7:30			655 Main Street
8:00	Special: Elephants at Home		Movie: *Mountain Home*
9:00	True Stories	Basketball Game of the Week	
10:00	The World Today		The News at Ten
10:30	Our City Today		Movie: *Dinner at Six*
11:00	Sports Summary		

> A: What time is "World News" on?
> B: It's on at 6:00.

9 Presentation

Questions with *How long . . . ?*

Use *How long . . . ?* to ask questions about the length of time an event lasts.

> A: "World of Sports" begins at 6:30. How long does it last?
> B: It lasts half an hour. It ends at 7:00.
> A: How long does the 7:00 movie last?
> B: It lasts two hours.

10 Practice

Choose a partner and ask and answer ten questions about the TV programs in *8*, or bring in a TV listing from an English-language newspaper. Use the models in *9*.

11 Listening

Number your paper from 1-10. Read the ad. Then listen to the conversation. Write *T* (true), *F* (false), or *NG* (not given).

> Large 4 bedroom house, 2 baths, modern kitchen, living room, family room, good location. No pets, no children under 10. $750/month plus utilities.
> Call Mr. King, (918) 522-0614.

1. Lisa is cleaning the kitchen and the living room.
2. Lisa is reading the newspaper.
3. The Logans want a new apartment.
4. The Logans visited five new houses.
5. Lisa saw an ad about a good house for rent.
6. The house in the ad was very small.
7. The rent for the house in the ad was reasonable.
8. The house for rent had a large garden.
9. The Logans liked the house.
10. Mr. and Mrs. Logan thanked Lisa.

12 Presentation

Learn to + verb; past tense of *become*

ONE-ON-ONE WITH SCOTT HAMILTON
by Susan Smith, Staff Reporter

Scott Hamilton, who won the gold medal at the 1984 Olympics in Lake Placid, New York, is in town this week. I asked him, "Why did you **learn to** ice skate?" Scott had a very unusual response. "I was always sick as a kid," he said. "I used to have a lot of bronchial infections. So, I **became** an ice skater because my doctor ordered me to start exercising on a regular basis. The cold air of the skating arena cleared up my breathing problems. Over the years, I **became** more and more interested in ice skating. It was no longer just a form of exercise."

So that was how Scott Hamilton **learned to** ice skate. He worked very hard and **became** a world class ice skater. You can see Scott perform in the Ice Show now playing at the Arena.

13 Practice

Make a statement using *learn to* and another sentence using *become*.

> Carlos / play soccer five years ago // good soccer player
>
> Carlos learned to play soccer five years ago.
> He became a good soccer player.

1. Gino / make Italian food in cooking school // excellent cook
2. Ana / swim the summer before last // pretty good swimmer
3. Liz / speak several languages // international telephone operator
4. Sam / fix cars in high school // mechanic
5. Sekila / ice skate last year // pretty good skater
6. Adela / write computer programs this year // computer programmer
7. Chang Ling / make sculptures fifteen years ago // famous sculptor
8. Cristina / swim when she was five // excellent swimmer
9. Joyce / play basketball when she was ten // good basketball player
10. Susan Smith / write in college // newspaper reporter

14 Writing

A.   Complete the ads below, using the words from the list.

1. beautiful	9. inexpensive	17. old
2. big	10. interesting	18. pretty
3. clean	11. large	19. private
4. excellent	12. long	20. public
5. expensive	13. marvelous	21. reasonable
6. good	14. modern	22. small
7. great	15. new	23. unbeatable
8. high	16. nice	24. wonderful

FOR SALE	FOR SALE	APARTMENT WANTED
_____ motorcycle. Looks _____ and is _____ to run. _____ price. Call 873-5942.	_____ house near _____ town. _____ trees, _____ area of land and _____ price. Must see this _____ place! For information, call 534-4876.	_____ family with _____ dog needs three _____ bedrooms, _____ kitchen, and _____ yard. Rent must be _____ . Call 233-0189.

B. Now write your own ad for something you would like to sell or something you want.

```



```

C. Exchange ads with a partner. Look at each other's ads, and then give them back. Take turns asking each other three or four questions about what you're selling.

15 Reading

Before You Read

1. What things do you like to do on weekends?

2. What kind of information about weekend events can you find in your newspaper?

First Reading

Read the following questions first, then scan "Weekend's Best" to answer the questions. *Scanning* means that you read quickly for specific information.

1. Name two free events.

2. Which two events have music?

3. Which is the most expensive event?

4. What events can you go to in the morning?

5. Which event has clowns?

6. Name three events for children.

WEEKEND'S BEST

SPECIAL EVENTS

MUSIC AT THE COURT

The Smithsonian's Palm Court Cameos music series pays tribute to Frank Loesser, who wrote songs such as "Baby, It's Cold Outside" and "Once in Love With Amy" and scores for such musicals as "Guys and Dolls." The free concerts are at noon Friday, and 1:30 and 3:30 Sunday at the Palm Court in the National Museum of Natural History, 12th Street and Constitution Avenue NW. Call 357-2700.

A DICKENS OF A PLAY

Scrooge, Tiny Tim, and all the marvelous characters of "A Christmas Carol" by Charles Dickens make their annual appearance at Ford's Theatre now through Dec. 31. Performances are at 7:30 Tuesday through Saturday, and 3:00 Sunday. Tickets are from $23 to $30; call 432-0200 or 800/448-9009. Ford's Theatre is at 511 10th St. NW.

KID STUFF

• **"Snow White,"** performed by the Atlanta Center for Puppetry Arts, lights up the Kennedy Center's Terrace Theater at 11:00, 1:30, and 3:30 Friday and Saturday, and 3:30 Sunday. Tickets are $8.50; call 467-4600.

• **"Les Ballons/The Balloon Show,"** an audience-participation clown show in French and English, is at the Capital Children's Museum, 800 Third St. NE, at 11:00 and 2:00 Friday and Saturday. Tickets to the show are $3, in addition to the regular museum fee of $5. Call 770-2937.

• Stella Stegosaurus, Dinah Diplodocus and the other talking and dancing dinosaurs of **"Dinosaur Rock"** perform this weekend. At 3:30 and 4:30 Sunday, the dinosaurs appear in the Alden Theatre at 1234 Ingleside Ave. in McLean. Tickets are $4.50; call 432-0200.

TOYS FOR TOTS

Mr. and Mrs. Claus and the Elves, the Marine Corps Color Guard, and some top-ranking Marines kick off the corps' annual Toys for Tots campaign with a tree-lighting ceremony at the Vista Hotel, 1400 M St. NW, at 3:00 Friday. Free, but bring a small, wrapped toy. Call 429-1700.

REST OF THE BEST

• **World Stamp Expo '89** continues at the Washington Convention Center, 11th Street and New York Avenue NW. Hours: 10 to 6 through Dec. 3. Admission is $2.50. Call 371-4200 . . .

• The **Potomac Depression Era Glass Show** is from 1:00 to 9:00 Friday, and 10:00 to 5:00 Saturday at Armory Place, Wayne Avenue and Fenton Street in Silver Spring. Admission $2; call 585-5564 . . .

• English, American, and Oriental antiques from the 18th and 19th centuries are on sale at the **Treasures and Pleasures of Christmas** show at the American University Sports Complex, Nebraska and Massachusetts Avenues NW. Show hours are 11:00 to 9:00 Friday through Sunday. Admission is $6. Call 244-1116.

Second Reading

Make a chart like the one below. Read "Weekend's Best" a second time and complete the chart with the correct information.

Type of Event	Day(s)	Time(s)	Place	Cost

16 Final Activity

Work with two classmates. Imagine that the Harris family is coming to visit you next weekend. Each person in the family likes to do different things. You want them to have a good time, so you look for things to do in the newspaper. Use the newspaper articles and ads in this unit, or use an English-language newspaper. Read about each person below and find at least two interesting things for each one to do. Explain why you think the person will enjoy these activities.

1. Mr. Harris is very tired. He wants to rest. At home he watches television a lot. He collects stamps, and he loves basketball.
2. Mrs. Harris likes to watch plays and listen to music. She also loves museums. She doesn't like restaurants.
3. Jenny Harris is 22. She just got a job in your city, and she's looking for an apartment. She loves Italian food, and she likes music, too.
4. Mark Harris is 18. He loves nice cars, but he doesn't have much money. He also loves literature. Dickens is his favorite author. He likes Mexican food.
5. Kate and Lucy are twins. They are 8 years old. They love stories and dancing. They also love dinosaurs.

Someday, I'll Be . . .

The Winfield Daily News has a section that includes today's horoscope, word games, and cartoons.

★ Your Stars Today ★

★ **Aries (March 21-April 19)**
Things are changing for the better. A new love will come into your life — be ready!

★ **Taurus (April 20-May 20)**
You'll make a lot of money if you're smart. Think about opening a part-time business.

★ **Gemini (May 21-June 21)**
Today is a lucky day for you. Listen to your friends. They'll give you good advice.

★ **Cancer (June 22-July 22)**
You'll meet a wonderful person in an unusual way, so be friendly to strangers.

★ **Leo (July 23-Aug. 22)**
An old friend will visit you and bring you a surprise.

★ **Virgo (Aug. 23-Sept. 22)**
Your fast thinking will be important in your work. Don't be afraid to give advice.

★ **Libra (Sept. 23-Oct. 23)**
Be prepared for new experiences. You'll travel to an interesting place soon.

★ **Scorpio (Oct. 24-Nov. 21)**
Something exciting will happen to you this afternoon. You'll get an important phone call.

★ **Sagittarius (Nov. 22-Dec. 21)**
Talk to your family about your problems — you won't be sorry. Don't be nervous about saying what you think.

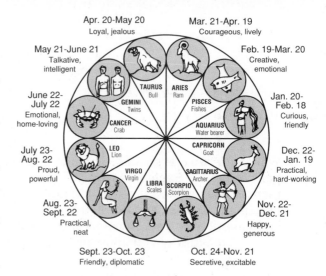

★ **Capricorn (Dec. 22-Jan. 19)**
Don't lose hope. There will be an important change in your life this week.

★ **Aquarius (Jan. 20-Feb. 18)**
Work hard this week — people are watching you. There is a promotion in your future.

★ **Pisces (Feb. 19-March 20)**
Save your money or you won't have it when you need it.

✎ FUN With Words

Word Search

Can you find twenty names of things you eat or drink?

```
S  P  A  G  H  E  T  T  I  J  O  S
A  W  A  T  E  R  E  L  M  E  M  A
L  I  F  K  L  R  A  P  P  L  E  U
A  L  N  O  F  I  S  H  O  G  A  C
D  E  S  S  E  R  T  I  T  U  T  E
T  R  U  F  U  T  O  M  A  T  O  P
C  I  G  P  I  Z  Z  A  T  L  K  H
O  R  A  N  G  E  Q  V  O  Z  R  B
F  I  R  H  A  M  B  U  R  G  E  R
F  C  B  U  T  T  E  R  H  C  A  E
E  E  H  W  R  S  M  O  L  S  V  A
E  X  T  L  A  G  R  A  P  E  S  D
```

SCRAMBLED WORDS

What words about sports can you make with these letters?

1. ETSAK
2. OCHCA
3. ETMA
4. ASBELLAB
5. WEMRSIM
6. CCOSRE
7. NERRNU
8. STENIN

1 Presentation

Talking about the future with *will*

Use **will** + *verb* to predict something or to say you are going to do something in the future.

Contractions with *will*

I will = I'll	we will = we'll
you will = you'll	
he will = he'll	they will= they'll
she will = she'll	
it will = it'll	

Useful vocabulary: probably = likely to be true

1. I really like science. Maybe I**'ll become** a doctor.
2. Be prepared for new experiences.
   You**'ll travel** to an interesting place soon.
3. An old friend is going to visit you. He**'ll bring** you a surprise.
4. It's cloudy today, but it**'ll be** sunny tomorrow.
5. We enjoyed our trip to California very much, so we**'ll** probably **go** there again in two or three years.
6. Listen to your friends. They**'ll give** you good advice.

2 Practice

Add an ending to each sentence using *but, will,* and *probably*. Make up your own ending for sentences 6-10.

> I'm sick today. / feel better tomorrow.
>
> I'm sick today, but I'll probably feel better tomorrow.

1. We're staying home this year. / take a long trip next year
2. I'm going to eat a lot tonight. / be sorry tomorrow
3. Gino wasn't very busy this morning. / have a lot of work tonight
4. You're going to the movies tonight. / stay at home on the weekend
5. Bob and Mike are nervous tonight. / do well on their test tomorrow
6. The weather is awful today. / . . .
7. I'm tired now. / . . .
8. Sam can't play soccer today. / . . .
9. We want to buy a new car this month. / . . .
10. You ate an enormous lunch. / . . .

3 Practice

Work with a partner. Use the information in *2*, but write *new* endings for the 10 sentences.

> I'm sick today, but I'll probably go to school tomorrow.

4 Reentry

Result clauses with *so*

Make a chart of your classmates' birthdays. Then look at the horoscope on page 28. Talk about a classmate's sign and future.

> Susana / October 20
>
> Susana was born on October 20, so she's a Libra. She'll travel to an interesting place soon. Maybe she'll go to Japan.

5 Presentation 📼

Negative statements with *will*

1. Cristina's sick. She **won't go** to the movies tonight.

2. Gino's parents probably **won't come** to the wedding because they live in Italy.

3. Talk to your family about your problems — you **won't be** sorry.

> **Contraction:**
> won't = will not

6 Practice

Make sentences with *won't*. A situation is given for each sentence. Think of as many logical predictions as possible for each sentence. You can use the *Suggestion Box*, or make up your own predictions.

> You don't like to type.
> You won't be happy at that job.

1. I have a doctor's appointment tomorrow.

2. She didn't like the salespeople at that store.

3. The Logans are going to the movies.

4. I don't want to go to that party.

5. Sam has to study.

6. You like to eat.

7. My favorite TV show is on tonight.

8. Carla's father has to work on Sundays.

9. Marion is very smart.

10. Bob wants to be with his friends on Saturday.

SUGGESTION BOX

be happy at that job
be at work
have a good time
ask someone to the movies
answer the telephone
study for the test
be at home tonight
have time to go to the movies
go on a diet
be home for dinner
shop there again

7 Vocabulary in Context

Talking about astrology

Astrologers look at the position of the **stars** in the **sky** at the time of your birth to tell your **future.** They make charts with information about your life. These charts are called **horoscopes.** Astrologers must know the date, time, and place of your birth to make a complete horoscope. You can find short horoscopes in many newspapers. Use your birthday to find your **sign** (Aries, etc.) in the newspaper, and then read the horoscope next to it.

8 Practice

Complete the paragraph with the following words. Change the form if necessary, and use each word only once.

astrologer	horoscope	sky
future	sign	star

Cristina bought a book on making (1) _____ by a famous (2) _____ . First she looked at a chart that showed the position of the (3) _____ in the (4) _____ when she was born. She read all about Gino's and her (5) _____ , Sagittarius and Aries, and now she thinks they're going to have a wonderful (6) _____ together.

9 Presentation

Irregular past tense: *find (out), lose, meet, pay, read, sell, think, wake up*

When I **woke up** this morning it was a beautiful, sunny day. I **read** my horoscope in the paper, and it said I was going to have a great day. I don't usually believe in horoscopes, but I **thought** today's horoscope was going to be different. It wasn't. First, I **lost** my car keys. I finally **found** them in the refrigerator! Second, I didn't meet someone wonderful. I **met** my new boss — he was awful! I didn't make a lot of money. I made a big mistake. I **sold** my car to a very nice man. Then I **found out** he **paid** me with a bad check. I'll never read my horoscope again!

10 Practice

Complete the following sentences with the past tense of verbs in *9*.

1. Last week I _____ my horoscope every day, and everything came true.

2. I _____ a marvelous woman.

3. I'm a car salesman. I _____ a lot of cars, and I made a lot of money.

4. I also _____ a diamond ring on the street!

5. When I _____ the next morning, I _____ about my good luck.

6. Then on Saturday, my horoscope said I was going to lose everything. And I did. I _____ my job!

7. Then I " _____ " my car. I went shopping and forgot where I parked it. It was two hours before I _____ my car!

8. Yesterday my horoscope said that I would help a stranger. In the afternoon I _____ an old man who was looking for a friend's house.

9. Together we _____ the house, but the friend wasn't at home.

10. So the old man had lunch at my house. I _____ that he's not a stranger after all. He knows my father!

11 Writing

Work in groups of three. Use the chart of birthdays that you made in *4* on page 30. Write horoscopes for your classmates like the ones in "Your Stars Today." Write one thing that each person *will* do in the future and one thing each person *will not* do in the future. Use what you know about each classmate to write your horoscopes! Share the horoscopes your group writes with the rest of the class.

Carlos / January 19

Carlos was born on January 19, so he's a Capricorn. This year he'll finish school, and he'll probably get a great job because he's smart. But he won't have a vacation, because he has to paint his apartment.

12 Interaction

Ask another student about the weather forecast.

A:	What's the weather forecast for	tomorrow?
		this weekend?

B:	Well, I just	heard	the forecast. It will _____	tomorrow.
		read		this weekend.

13 Presentation

Questions and short answers with *will*

Short Answers:

Yes, I will.
No, I won't.

A

A: Will you please call me tomorrow?
B: Yes, I will.

B

A: Will Roberto go to class tonight?
B: No, he won't.

14 Practice

Work with a partner. Take turns asking and answering questions with *will*. You decide whether to answer *yes* or *no*.

your friends / visit you next year
A: Will your friends visit you next year?
B: Yes, they will.

you / see your family soon
A: Will you see your family soon?
B: No, I won't.

1. you / graduate next year
2. your parents / visit you next month
3. your friends / invite you to the movies tomorrow

4. your teacher / give you homework tonight
5. your friend / have dinner with you tomorrow night
6. we / go shopping on Saturday
7. I / see you on Sunday
8. you / be at the library Friday night
9. we / get our new books next week
10. I / have time to finish my homework this afternoon

15 Practice

Work with a partner. One student is a fortune teller. The other student asks questions about the future. Be sure to use *will* in the questions. The fortune teller answers with short answers and adds a statement.

> Cristina / meet Gino's parents // yes // visit them in Italy
> YOU: Will Cristina meet Gino's parents?
> FORTUNE TELLER: Yes, she will. She'll visit them in Italy.

1. Adela / get a job // yes // work as a computer programmer
2. Sam and Bob / play soccer next week // yes // play in the park
3. Mike / go to Mexico again this year // no // go next year
4. Hajime Ito / be in the next race // yes // probably win a medal
5. the history test / be easy // no // have a lot of hard questions
6. the weather / be nice tomorrow // . . . // . . .
7. I / be rich // . . . // . . .
8. I / go to . . . // . . . // . . .
9. the next test / . . . // . . . // . . .
10. . . . // become famous // . . .

16 Interaction

Ask another student about future plans.

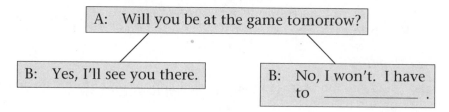

A: Will you be at the game tomorrow?

B: Yes, I'll see you there.

B: No, I won't. I have to _____ .

17 Presentation

Information questions with *will*

A: Who will I meet?
B: You'll meet a famous person.
A: Where will I travel?
B: You'll travel to Australia.
A: When will I travel to Australia?
B: In 1995.

18 Practice

Interview two classmates to find out the answers to the following questions. Then share the information with the class.

1. Where will you be living in 10 years?
2. What will you be doing?
3. Who will you be living with?

19 Listening

Number your paper from 1-10. Look at the list of radio programs. Then listen and write the letter of the program you hear.

a. "Local News"
b. "Sports Report"
c. "At the Movies"
d. "Restaurant Review"
e. "News Around the World"
f. "Business Today"
g. "Advice from Ann"
h. "Weather Report"
i. "Your Stars Today"
j. "Help Wanted"

20 Reading

Before You Read

1. What do you know about the stars?
2. Do you think astrology is a true science?
3. What do astronomers do?

First Reading

Read "Studying the Stars" to find out similarities and differences between astrology and astronomy.

Studying the Stars

Most of us enjoy looking up at the night sky on a clear night and seeing thousands upon thousands of twinkling stars. Human beings have always been fascinated by the stars in the sky above. These glittering points of light are romantic and mysterious to many of us, but for some people they[1] are important objects of study. These people are astronomers and astrologers.

Astrologers study the stars to predict what is going to happen in a person's life, while astronomers study them to find out about the universe, the sun, other stars, and the planets. Hundreds of years ago, many famous astronomers also gave astrological advice. For early man, the sky was extremely important because both the sun and the rain came from the sky. Priests observed and studied the sky so they could give advice about the best time for planting and harvesting crops. Through their[2] observations, many important discoveries were made. For example, they[3] developed calendars and learned how to predict eclipses. Rulers and kings asked for advice from these early priest-astronomers. They[4] often asked them[5] to predict future events, such as the result of a battle. Early astronomers began to predict future events of all kinds, and this is how astrology started.

Astrologers study the position of the stars and planets at the time of a person's birth, and then tell what will happen in a person's life. They[6] study the position of the stars, in order to predict the future. These predictions are called horoscopes, and many people today believe that they[7] should look at their horoscope every day. Great rulers in history, and even important people in our own time believe that the advice of astrologers is important.

Early astrologers and astronomers could only study the stars with their[8] eyes. The invention of telescopes made it possible to study the stars better, and astronomy began to develop as a science. Astronomers observed the positions of the stars and the movement of the earth and other planets in space. From these observations, they[9] began to understand scientific laws (such as gravity), and they disproved some old ideas, such as, the earth being the center of the universe! Today, astronomy is an important science and has greatly expanded our knowledge of the universe. We know, for example, that the earth is very small compared to other objects in space. It[10] is only one of the planets that revolves around our star, the sun. And the sun is just one of billions of stars in our galaxy, which is just one of millions of galaxies in the universe.

So, although astrology and astronomy both study the stars and started at about the same time in history, today they[11] are quite different.

Second Reading

A. **Look at the numbered pronouns. Write the noun that each pronoun refers to. The first one is done for you as an example.**

1. they   *stars*
2. their
3. they
4. They
5. them
6. They
7. they
8. their
9. they
10. It
11. they

B. Read "Studying the Stars" again to compare and contrast astrologers and astronomers. Make a compare/contrast table like the one below, then work with two or three classmates to complete it. Share your group's compare/contrast table with other groups.

STUDYING THE STARS — COMPARE/CONTRAST TABLE

Questions to Ask:	ASTROLOGERS	ASTRONOMERS
What do astrologers and astronomers do?		
Why do they study the stars?		
Is their work important? Why/Why not?		

21 Final Activity

Write three sentences about what you will do in the future. One sentence tells *who* you will meet or marry, one sentence tells *what* will happen to you in the year 2000, and one sentence tells *where* you will go. Write each one on a separate piece of paper and fold the papers so no one can see your sentences.

> I will marry a famous actor/actress.

> I will win a million dollars in the year 2000.

> I will travel to the South Pole.

Collect the folded papers in three boxes labeled: *who, what, where.* Work in pairs. One person is the fortune teller. The fortune teller chooses a folded paper from each box. Role play a dialogue between the fortune teller and a customer. Then reverse roles.

> A: Ask who you will meet.
> B: Answer, using information from one of the folded papers.
> A: Ask what will happen to you in the year 2000.
> B: Answer, using information from one of the folded papers.
> A: Ask where you will travel.
> B: Answer, using information from one of the folded papers.

COMMUNICATION
Talking about past events ▪ Disagreeing
GRAMMAR
There was/there were ▪ Past continuous: statements and questions ▪ Clauses with *when* and *while* ▪ The emphatic *do*

SKILLS
Reading newspaper headlines ▪ Listening to news reports ▪ Writing a news report

Fire at the Plaza

Every night the evening news on TV begins with an important story. Tonight the news describes a big fire.

"This is Bruce Ward for WNFD News. There was a serious fire at the Plaza Hotel this afternoon. It started at 3:10 in the kitchen on the first floor.

"When reporters arrived at the hotel at 3:25, the first and second floors were on fire, and smoke was coming from the third- and fourth-floor windows. People were standing at the windows and yelling for help, and firefighters were using ladders to rescue them.

"Some people had bad burns, and ambulances arrived to take them to the hospital. While firefighters were rescuing guests, one man jumped from a second-floor window and broke his leg.

"By 4:00 the fire was under control. The cause of the fire is still unknown."

Vocabulary in Context

Talking about a fire

Read the news report again and match the words to their definitions.

1. serious ___	**a.** a car or van that takes people to the hospital
2. ladder ___	**b.** an injury from a fire
3. yell ___	**c.** stop from becoming bigger
4. smoke ___	**d.** burning
5. rescue ___	**e.** a horizontal part of a building
6. ambulance ___	**f.** throw yourself into the air
7. jump ___	**g.** a thing with steps that can be moved
8. on fire ___	**h.** stop somebody from dying or being hurt
9. burn ___	**i.** very bad
10. floor ___	**j.** something like a cloud that comes from a fire
11. window ___	**k.** a glass part in a wall
12. control ___	**l.** speak loudly

2 Presentation

Talking about past events with *there was* and *there were*

Now	Yesterday
1. There is a serious fire at the Plaza Hotel.	**There was** a serious fire at the Plaza Hotel.
2. There are three fire trucks at the fire.	**There were** three fire trucks at the fire.

3 Practice

Look at the following headlines from yesterday's newspaper. Tell what happened using *there was* and *there were*.

Bank Robbery in Middletown
June 10—A bank robber entered the Middletown National Bank

> There was a bank robbery in Middletown.

1.

Big Sale at Warner's
June 10—The doors to Warner's Department Store will open at eight

2.

Swimming Races at Winfield High
June 10—Middletown and Winfield students are competing in the New York

3.

Party for President at Plaza Hotel
June 10—Local city leaders attended a party for the President

4.

Three Fires in Westlake
June 10—A child died and a fire-fighter was injured

5.

Wedding at St. Mark's Church
June 10—Frank Romero and Rosa Martinez were wed yesterday

6.

Important Meeting in Paris
June 10—Washington, D.C.—The President returned from Paris today after meeting with European leaders

7.

Rock Concert at Riverview Stadium
June 10—Last night's concert by the talented rock group

8.

Plane Crash
June 10—Municipal Airport—A small plane missed the airport runway late last night and crashed into a

4 Presentation

Questions and short answers with _there was_ and _there were_

A
A: Was there a wedding at St. Mark's Church?
B: Yes, **there was.**

B
A: Was there an important meeting in Hartford?
B: No, **there wasn't.**

C
A: Were there any Winfield students in the swimming finals?
B: Yes, **there were.**

D
A: Were there six fires in Westlake?
B: No, **there weren't.**

5 Practice

Work with a partner. Use the cues to ask and answer questions about the information in the newspaper headlines in _3_.

a bank robbery in Winfield?

A: Was there a bank robbery in Winfield yesterday?
B: No, there wasn't. There was a bank robbery in Middletown.

1. a big sale at Lawrence's?

2. any baseball games?

3. a meeting in Paris?

4. a plane crash last night?

5. a party at Winfield High?

6. a wedding announcement in the paper?

7. any fires in Westlake?

8. a jazz concert in Riverview?

6 Practice

Look at the picture and then read the story below. Complete the story using words from *1*. Change the form of the word if necessary.

Yesterday there was a (1) _____ fire at the Plaza Hotel. Elvira Johnson was working on the third (2) _____ when the fire started in the kitchen on the first floor. She saw (3) _____ coming from the (4) _____ . She told everybody to leave the building. Then she called the fire department to tell them that the building was (5) _____ .

When the firefighters arrived, people were yelling for help from the windows. Some firefighters began to (6) _____ the fire, and other firefighters climbed (7) _____ to (8) _____ people on the second and third floors. Some people were afraid and they (9) _____ from the windows. Five people had bad (10) _____ and went to the hospital by (11) _____ .

Imagine that you are walking in front of the Plaza Hotel with a friend the day after the fire. You did not know there was a fire there yesterday but your friend saw it. Work with a partner. Practice a conversation using the following instructions.

A: Point out the building and ask about the fire.
(Hey, look at that building! Was there a fire?)
B: Answer the question and tell about the size of the fire.
A: Ask if your friend saw the fire.
B: Answer "yes" and tell your friend you were in the restaurant across the street.
A: Ask where the fire started.
B: Answer and say that there was a lot of smoke.
A: Ask if there were any ambulances there.
B: Answer "yes."
A: Ask if anybody was hurt.
B: Answer "yes" and say how many people went to the hospital by ambulance.
A: Ask if your friend was afraid.
B: Answer and tell about the people in the building.

8 Presentation

Talking about past events: past continuous statements

> The past continuous consists of **was/were** + *verb*-**ing**.
> It describes an action that was taking place at a specific moment in time.

1. At 3:25 smoke **was coming** from the windows.
2. During the rescue people **were standing** at the windows.

9 Practice

Use past continuous verbs to describe events at the Plaza. Choose a verb that makes sense in each sentence.

> That morning Elvira . . . on the third floor.
>
> That morning Elvira was working on the third floor.

1. At 3:25 people . . . at the windows.
2. Firefighters . . . guests.
3. People . . . for help.
4. Ambulances . . . people to the hospital.
5. A news photographer . . . pictures.
6. Firefighters . . . ladders.
7. Guests and hotel workers . . . from the building.
8. A rescue worker . . . people with burns.

10 Presentation

Asking about past events: past continuous questions

1. Was a photographer taking pictures during the fire?

2. Were rescue workers helping people with burns?

3. Who was rescuing the guests?

4. What was coming from the windows?

5. Who were the firefighters rescuing?

6. What were the firefighters using to rescue people?

7. Where were the ambulances taking people?

11 Practice

Make at least two past continuous questions from each sentence in *9*.

> Was Elvira working on the third floor that morning?
>
> Where was Elvira working that morning?

12 Practice

Look at the picture of the fire on page 43. Ask and answer questions using the past continuous.

> A: Where were the guests standing?
> B: They were standing at the windows.

13 Presentation

Past continuous statements; clauses with *when*

> 1. We **were eating** dinner at the hotel **when** somebody **yelled,** "Fire!"
> 2. **When** reporters **arrived** at the fire, smoke **was coming** from the third- and fourth-floor windows.

14 Practice

Change each sentence to the past continuous tense. Begin each sentence with *When the reporters got to the hotel . . .*

> A lot of people watched the fire.
>
> When the reporters got to the hotel, a lot of people were watching the fire.

1. A rescue worker helped some people with bad burns.
2. A firefighter climbed a ladder.
3. The firefighters tried to control the fire.
4. Some guests ran from the building.
5. Some guests stood at the windows.
6. A photographer took pictures of the fire.
7. Smoke came from the windows.
8. Firefighters looked for a little girl.
9. An old man yelled for help.
10. The first ambulance arrived.

15 **Presentation** 🔲

Interrupted actions vs. continuous actions

Use clauses with **while** to talk about interrupted actions or continuous actions.

Interrupted actions:

simple past	**while** + past continuous

OR

while + past continuous	simple past

The fire started while the cooks were preparing dinner for a private party.

While the cooks were preparing dinner for a private party, the fire started.

Continuous actions:

while + past continuous	past continuous

While firefighters were rescuing guests, police officers were controlling traffic around the hotel.

16 **Practice**

Complete the sentences with the past or past continuous form of the verb.

While we ___*were waiting*___ for the 3:00 train, a man ___*announced*___
        (wait)   (announce)
that all trains ___*were running*___ late; so we ___*took*___ the bus.
            (run)   (take)

1. While I _____ tennis, it _____ to rain; so
            (play)   (start)
I _____ home.
    (come)

2. Lisa _____ a pencil while she _____ her
            (break)   (do)
homework.

3. Bob _____ Mike to go to the lake, but Mike _____ ;
  (ask)   (study)

so Bob _____ another friend.
  (call)

4. When Mike _____ home, Liz _____ on the
  (get)   (talk)

telephone.

5. Ted and Joyce _____ in the yard. Elinor _____
  (work)   (say)

dinner was ready, so they _____ into the house.
  (go)

6. While the Itos _____ in Europe, they _____
  (travel)   (visit)

many museums.

7. I _____ lunch when I _____ my old teacher.
  (eat)   (see)

She still _____ the same.
  (look)

8. Akiko _____ to the store when she _____ an
  (drive)   (have)

accident. She _____ too fast.
  (go)

9. Ahmed _____ while his wife _____ a shower.
  (cook)   (take)

10. A man _____ while we _____ to listen.
  (talk)   (try)

17 Presentation

Disagreeing

> Use the emphatic **do** to disagree.

A
A: Many senators don't like President Brackston.
B: That's not true. Many **do** like him.

B
A: President Brackston doesn't help poor people.
B: What do you mean? He **does** help poor people.

C	
A:	The firefighters didn't have a lot to do.
B:	That's not true. They **did** have a lot to do.

D	
A:	The fire didn't start in the kitchen.
B:	What do you mean? It **did** start in the kitchen.

18 Practice

You are talking with some friends about the coming election. You have different opinions. Disagree with each sentence. Use the models in *17*.

1. Senator Tunnel doesn't work hard for peace.
2. He didn't do a lot in the Senate.
3. He doesn't want to help poor people.
4. The Senator doesn't want to have a strong army.
5. He doesn't know how to be a leader.
6. The other senators don't like working with him.
7. President Brackston doesn't work well with other leaders.
8. The President doesn't understand the Senate.
9. He didn't cut our taxes like he promised.
10. He didn't want to give money for cleaning the air.

19 Interaction

Pretend you're a parent having an argument with your child.

P:	"You don't help around the house."
C:	"I *do* help. I wash the dishes."

P:	Say the child doesn't help around the house.
C:	Disagree and say you do the laundry.
P:	Say the child doesn't study.
C:	Disagree and say you were studying all night last night.
P:	Say the child doesn't save any money.
C:	Disagree and say you have $200 in the bank.
P:	Say the child doesn't clean his/her room.
C:	Disagree and say you cleaned it two days ago.

20 Listening

Number your paper from 1-10. Listen to the interview and write *T* (true), *F* (false), or *NG* (not given) for each sentence.

1. Jim Molloy is a reporter for the *Winfield News*.
2. Jim rescued a small girl named Janice from the fire.
3. Janice's brother was crying because he had a bad burn.
4. Janice's brother didn't know where his sister was.
5. Jim had to go to the hospital because he had serious burns.
6. Janice was sick from the smoke.
7. Janice didn't leave the house because she was afraid.
8. Janice is going to be OK.
9. Janice is still in the hospital.
10. Jim didn't take any pictures of the fire.

21 Reading

Before You Read

1. Do you know how to get help in an emergency?
2. Do you know how you can give help in an emergency?

Work with a partner. Student 1 reads the first reading selection ("Accident? Injury? Illness?") and Student 2 reads the second reading selection ("Become a Volunteer"). Student 1 then asks Student 2 the questions in *A*, and Student 2 asks Student 1 the questions in *B*.

EMERGENCY
Dial 911
Montgomery County
Dial 652-1000
Upper Northwest, D.C.

NON-EMERGENCY
Dial 652-0077

ACCIDENT? INJURY? ILLNESS?

A PHONE CALL to one of these numbers brings you help immediately. All of the resources of the Rescue Squad go into action to help you and your neighbors. After making the call, here are some things you or a neighbor can do to help us get to your emergency quickly:

• Turn on your outside light.
• Have someone stand outside to guide us.
• If you live in an apartment building with a desk clerk or a security guard, have them make sure the front door is unlocked and there is an elevator waiting on the lobby floor.
• If there is no clerk or security guard, ask a neighbor to go down and unlock the door and wait to guide us to your apartment.

BECOME A VOLUNTEER

YOU ARE THE RESCUE SQUAD! More than 150 Rescue Squad members put in thousands of hours of volunteer time to make sure we are ready to handle every call for help. You can be a part of this dedicated group. If you are 18 or older, a high school graduate and have some spare time, consider becoming a Rescue Squad member. If you are between 16 and 18, look into our Junior Membership program. You will receive training and experience, and when you reach 18 you will be eligible for full membership. The community's financial support has always been appreciated. Now, GIVE OF YOURSELF! For more information, contact the Membership Committee at 652-0077.

After You Read

A. Student 1 asks Student 2 these questions:

1. How many people work in the Rescue Squad?
2. What qualifications do you need to work in the Rescue Squad?
3. Can a 17-year-old help in the Rescue Squad?
4. Do people in the Rescue Squad get paid?

B. Student 2 asks Student 1 these questions:

1. What number do you call if you have an emergency and you live in Montgomery County?
2. What number do you call if you want information about the Rescue Squad?
3. What can you do to help the Rescue Squad find your house?
4. If you live in an apartment building, what can you do to help the Rescue Squad find your apartment?

22 Writing

The photograph below shows the Rescue Squad getting an injured man out of a car accident. Write a paragraph describing the accident, how the Rescue Squad was called, what they did when they arrived, and what happened to the man. Remember to tell *who, when, what, where, how,* and *why.*

Ask your partner to read your paragraph and note any suggestions for change. Then rewrite your paragraph.

23 Final Activity

Pretend that you and a friend were driving on a highway when you saw a bad accident happen. Several cars were in the accident. There was a fire, and people were injured. Firefighters, ambulances, and police arrived at the scene.

Work in groups of three. One person is a police officer. He/she is interviewing the other two people — the *witnesses.* The police officer needs to find out this information:

- What time did the accident happen?
- Where were the witnesses?
- How many cars were there in the accident? (Did any cars in the accident drive away before the police arrived?)
- What did the drivers of the cars in the accident do?
- Where did the fire start?
- Who called for help?
- Who arrived first, the firefighters or the ambulances?

The two witnesses are too nervous to remember *exactly* what they saw. They disagree, and give different answers to the police officer's questions. (Remember: Use the emphatic *do* to disagree.)

UNIT 5

COMMUNICATION
Reading and discussing newspaper headlines and articles ▪ Agreeing and disagreeing

GRAMMAR
Irregular past tense: *steal, catch* ▪ Position of adverbs of frequency with verbs ▪ *It's +* adjective + *to* + verb ▪ Indefinite pronouns: *something, anything, nothing* ▪ Irregular plurals

SKILLS
Reading a letter to the editor ▪ Writing a letter to the editor

Look At These Headlines!

Gloria and Sekila are reading the Sunday newspaper.

GLORIA: Look at these headlines! Robbers, muggers — it's the same thing every day.

SEKILA: Yeah. And the police aren't doing anything about it.

GLORIA: But what *can* they do? It's impossible to control crime.

SEKILA: Sometimes I think it's better not to read the newspaper.

'Many unanswered questions' in baby's death from formula

by Loretta McLaughlin
GLOBE STAFF

The mystery surrounding the death Monday of an 11-month-old baby at Children's Hospital Medical Center deepened yesterday as no firm leads developed to explain how excessive salt was mixed into the infant formula that killed him.

Dorchester man shot twice in leg by four robbers

Four young men entered a Dorchester man's apartment at 2 PM yesterday, police said, and within 10 minutes shot him twice and stole a home computer, a television set, a stereo system, a cassette player, and an undetermined amount of cash.

Man charged in murder of mother, twin brother

SPRINGFIELD - A man who neighbors said devoted his life to

Body found in Springfield

Springfield Police yesterday were trying to identify a middle-aged man found dead in a vacant apartment building, and the cause of death. The fully-clothed man was found on the top floor of an empty four-story apartment building on Patton Street at about 4:30 AM, after police received an anonymous tip. Detective Capt. Ernest M. Stelzer said there were no visible wounds or marks on the man's body except a scratch over one eye, and he was carrying

1 Vocabulary in Context

Talking about crime; irregular past tense: *steal, catch*

A

"Give us all of the money!"

Three men **robbed** a bank.

B

"I'll get them!"

They **stole** $10,000.

C

"I got you!"

Officer Mann **caught** one bank robber. The other two **escaped**.

D

"Oh, no!"

The **officer** took the **robber** to **jail**.

2 Practice

Complete the news story using words from *1*. Change the form of the word if necessary.

WESTERN BANK ROBBED

There was another crime in El Paso last night. Three men (1) _____ the Western Bank and (2) _____ $10,000. A county police (3) _____ (4) _____ one of the men and put him in (5) _____, but the other two (6) _____ escaped in a light blue car. These men (7) _____ people and (8) _____ for a living. They are very dangerous.

Reading news headlines

Headlines give the important information in newspaper articles. They are not complete sentences, so they don't have words like **a, the, and, but, there, is, were, his, her,** and **their.**

Headlines use verbs ending with **-ing** to tell about present events.

More Students Traveling to Europe

September 9—More students are traveling to Europe this year because of low airfares.

Headlines use present tense verbs to tell about past events.

Firefighter Rescues Child From Hotel Fire

January 17—A firefighter rescued a child from a fire at the Plaza Hotel last night.

Headlines use verbs with **to** to tell about future events.

City to Open New Community College

August 3—The city will open a new community college in the fall.

4 Practice

A. Read each headline and choose the sentence that best describes it.

> FIRE CLOSES WESTLAKE HIGH SCHOOL FOR WEEK
> **a.** A fire closed Westlake High School for a week.
> **b.** A fire will close Westlake High School next week.
> **c.** A fire will close Westlake High School for a week.

1. THOUSANDS OF TOURISTS TO VISIT EUROPE
   a. Thousands of tourists visited Europe.
   b. Thousands of tourists will visit Europe.
   c. Thousands of tourists are visiting Europe now.

2. ORANGES FREEZING IN FLORIDA SNOW
   a. Oranges froze in the Florida snow.
   b. Oranges will freeze in the Florida snow.
   c. Oranges are freezing in the Florida snow now.

3. PLAYER BREAKS LEG, TEAM STILL WINS
   a. A player broke his leg, but his team won the game.
   b. A player will break his leg, but his team will win the game.
   c. A player just broke his leg, but his team is winning the game now.

4. MAN WITH TEN CHILDREN TO MARRY WOMAN WITH EIGHT
   a. A man with ten children married a woman with eight.
   b. A man with ten children will marry a woman with eight.
   c. A man with ten children is marrying a woman with eight now.

5. PRESIDENT RETURNS FROM MOSCOW
   a. The President returned from Moscow.
   b. The President will return from Moscow.
   c. The President is returning from Moscow now.

B. **Write your own sentences to describe each of these headlines:**

1. PLANE CRASHES, PILOT OK

2. PRINCE OF ENGLAND TO MARRY MOVIE STAR

3. "OTHELLO" OPENING AT GLOBE THEATER

4. MAN ROBS SUPERMARKET

5. BIG SNOWSTORM COMING

5 Interaction

Work with a partner. Each student should read the headlines in an English-language newspaper. (If you do not have an English-language newspaper, look at a local paper and comment in English on the headlines.) Then exchange newspapers and talk about them. Here are some suggestions to help you start your conversation.

A: Hey! Did you see this headline? It says . . . .
B: Oh, yeah. I saw that story. It's about . . . .

A: Say, this is interesting. There's an article about . . . .
B: Really? I didn't see that one. What does it say?

A: Here's an interesting headline: . . . .
B: Now that is interesting. What does the article say?

6 Presentation

Position of adverbs of frequency with verbs

> Note the position of adverbs of frequency with verbs:
>
> subject + adverb + verb

Adverbs of frequency:	
always	sometimes
usually	rarely
often	never

1. **She always works** after school.
2. **He never gets** up early.
3. **I sometimes work** on weekends.

Sometimes can also be placed at the beginning or end of the sentence:

4. **Sometimes** I work on weekends.
5. I work on weekends **sometimes**.

7 Practice

A newspaper in Atlanta asked people about the articles they read. Read the information in the chart below and make sentences about how often the people read different kinds of articles.

> The people always read the headlines.

READER QUESTIONNAIRE: Summary of 100 respondents

DO YOU READ ...	Always	Usually	Often	Sometimes	Rarely	Never
Headlines	X					
Sports			X			
International News			X			
Local News		X				
TV Guide		X				
Arts					X	
Movie Guide			X			
Letters to the Editor				X		
Horoscope		X				
Advice Column				X		
Comics	X					
Science News					X	
Garden News				X		
Classified Ads				X		
Births and Deaths						X

Practice

Read each sentence, and look at the time clue in parentheses. Then make a sentence using *never, rarely, sometimes, often, usually,* or *always.*

> Sam Logan works from 8:00 AM to 5:00 PM. (Monday through Friday)
>
> Sam Logan always works from 8:00 AM to 5:00 PM.

1. Sam goes to school after work. (Monday, Tuesday)
2. He studies late at night. (Monday, Tuesday, Wednesday, Thursday)
3. He has free time during the weekend. (three weekends a month)
4. He goes to the movies during the week. (0)
5. He stays at home on Saturday. (52 times a year)
6. He eats dinner at an expensive restaurant. (3 times a year)
7. He visits his girlfriend on Sunday. (every Sunday)
8. He goes on dates with her on Fridays. (3 times a month)
9. He buys clothes. (once or twice a year)
10. He watches sports on TV when he's at his girlfriend's house. (every time he's there)

9 Reentry

And so + *do/does/did* + noun

A group of people at a party are talking about their children, relatives, and friends. Make sentences to see what they are saying about everyone.

> My friend wants to learn English. / I
> My friend wants to learn English, and so do I.

1. Joyce wrote a letter to her pen pal. / Ana
2. The Navas like to travel. / the Youngs
3. Hajime and Mario visited Santa Fe. / Carlos and Ana
4. Steve and Maria got married. / Paul and Annette
5. Tom reads the newspaper every day. / Adela and Lisa
6. Sam and Bob go to the park on Saturdays. / Mike
7. Cristina studies at Winfield Community College. / Sekila
8. Cristina always gets good grades. / Sekila
9. I want to go to France this year. / my brother and sister
10. I have to get up early tomorrow. / my parents

10 Presentation

It's + adjective + to + verb

> 1. **It's impossible to** control crime.
> 2. **It's important to** read newspapers.
> 3. **It's good to** like your work.
> 4. **It's expensive to** take a vacation.

11 Practice

Match the adjectives and phrases below to make sentences.

> It's great to see you again.

1. great		**a.**	drive there in three hours
2. impossible		**b.**	see you again
3. good		**c.**	fly there from here
4. sad		**d.**	be here
5. possible		**e.**	read about computers
6. wonderful		**f.**	work and go to school at night
7. expensive		**g.**	go to New York for a vacation
8. boring		**h.**	read the comics
9. hard		**i.**	get pictures from friends
10. important		**j.**	be on time for meetings
11. dumb		**k.**	forget your ticket
12. nice		**l.**	hear bad news

12 Presentation

Indefinite pronouns *something, anything, nothing*

Lisa is babysitting for the Hills. Here is a conversation between her and the children.

ERIK: We're bored. There's **nothing** to do.
ANN: Is there **anything** on TV?
ERIK: Nah! There isn't **anything** on TV.
LISA: Would you like **something** to eat?
ERIK: No! We want to do **something** fun!
ANN: Yeah!

13 Practice

Complete the conversation that takes place when the parents get home. Use *something*, *anything*, or *nothing*.

MRS. HILL: Did _____ exciting happen while we were away?
ERIK: No! _____ happened.
ANN: We didn't have _____ to do.
LISA: I wanted to give them _____ to eat . . .
MR. HILL: Was there _____ in the refrigerator?
LISA: Well, I couldn't find _____ .
MRS. HILL: Oh, dear! There's _____ in the refrigerator. I forgot
to go shopping.
MR. HILL: You must all be very hungry. Let's all go out and get
_____ to eat. Lisa, can you come with us?
LISA: I'd like to, thanks. But I have _____ to do tonight.
MR. HILL: Well, next time then.
MRS. HILL: Lisa, next time there will be _____ in the refrigerator.
I promise!

14 Interaction

Work with a partner. Ask and answer questions about the past.

A: Did you do anything | yesterday?
                        | last weekend?

B: No, there was nothing to do.

B: Yes, I _____ .

15 Presentation

Irregular plurals

> Some nouns that end in **-f** or **-fe** have irregular plurals.
> In these nouns the **-f/-fe** changes to **-ves.**
>
> | -f/-fe ⟶ | -ves | BUT | -f ⟶ | -fs |
> |---|---|---|---|---|
> | wife ⟶ | wives | | roof ⟶ | roofs |
> | knife ⟶ | knives | | belief ⟶ | beliefs |
> | loaf ⟶ | loaves | | chef ⟶ | chefs |
> | scarf ⟶ | scarves | | chief ⟶ | chiefs |
> | thief ⟶ | thieves | | | |
> | leaf ⟶ | leaves | | | |
> | wolf ⟶ | wolves | | | |

Remember:

child ⟶ children
man ⟶ men
woman ⟶ women

Useful vocabulary:

1. **thief** = robber
2. **leaf** =
3. **wolf** = wild animal, like a dog
4. **roof** = top of a building
5. **chef** = cook

1. Oh, no! The child has a **knife!**
2. **Children** must not play with **knives.**

16 Practice

Change the words in dark print to the plural. Make any other necessary changes.

> The **man** has a **knife.**
>
> The men have knives.

1. The **man** went to the party with his **wife** and **child**.
2. The **loaf** of bread was very old.
3. In the winter, the **woman** wears a wool **scarf**.
4. The **chef** used a **knife** to cut the bread.
5. The **boy** talked about the **wolf** he saw at the National Park.
6. The **thief** robbed a bank.
7. In November, the last **leaf** fell from the tree.
8. This winter **I** fixed the **roof** on the house.

17 Listening 🔲

First Listening

Number your paper from 1-5. Listen to each news story and write the letter of the correct headline.

1. **a.** POLICE CATCH BANK ROBBERS
   b. BANK ROBBERS ESCAPE
2. **a.** MIKE O'BRIEN WINS SWIMMING RACE
   b. JAPANESE SWIMMER BEATS CANADIAN
3. **a.** PRESIDENT ON EUROPEAN TRIP
   b. PRESIDENT HOME FROM EUROPE
4. **a.** LARGE FIRE IN FRENCH RESTAURANT
   b. GUESTS ESCAPE LARGE FIRE AT PLAZA
5. **a.** GINO LEONE PREPARES ITALIAN DINNER
   b. GINO LEONE AND CRISTINA SILVA ANNOUNCE WEDDING
       NEXT FALL

Second Listening

Number your paper from 1-5 again. Listen to the news stories a second time and answer the questions.

1. **a.** How many robbers were there?
   b. How much money did they steal?
2. **a.** How long was the race?
   b. When was the race?
3. **a.** Where is the President now?
   b. How many other countries did he visit?
4. **a.** How much damage was there from the Plaza Hotel fire?
   b. How many people were hurt?
5. **a.** Who is getting married?
   b. When will the wedding take place?

18 Reading

Before You Read

1. Do you read the "Letters to the Editor" section of the newspaper?
2. Do you write letters to the editor sometimes? If so, why?
3. Why do you think people write letters to the editor?

First Reading

Think of the following questions as you read the letter from Sandra Smith to the editor of the *Westlake Herald*. After you read the letter, work in small groups and discuss the answers.

1. Why does Ms. Smith think that Morton Prison is a bad place?
2. What is her opinion of criminals?
3. What suggestion does Ms. Smith make to solve the problems at Morton?
4. Do you agree with Ms. Smith? Why or why not?

Letters to the Editor

Morton Prison: a disgrace

I am absolutely furious. Morton Prison is an absolute disgrace. A robber or a mugger is sentenced and is put in Morton for 20 or 25 years, and what happens? After a few years of so-called "good behavior" he can work outside the prison or go home for the weekend. And what does he do then? Commits more crimes, of course. Every day there are newspaper headlines, such as: "Prisoner on Work Release Robs Bank," or "Convicted Mugger on Weekend Visit Attacks Woman." These are dangerous criminals. They should not be given opportunities to commit more crimes. What is the matter with the prison authorities at Morton? Do they really think that a few years of prison life will reform hardened criminals who rob, steal, and kill? Don't they understand that it is impossible to change criminals?

I have been a police officer for 25 years, and I know what the criminal mind is like: cruel and usually crazy. But the do-gooders at Morton Prison have the naive idea that they can change their prisoners and make them into useful members of society. Security is so bad at Morton that prisoners can escape without much trouble. Just look at the headlines: "Four Prisoners Climb Wall to Escape Morton — No Clues." And what do the Morton authorities say? "Well, it's Christmas — they probably wanted to go home."

What I say is, put the criminals behind bars and throw away the key. It's the only way to protect people from violent crime.

SANDRA SMITH
Riverview

Second Reading

Scan the reading a second time to find the words listed on the left below. Use the context to choose the best synonym or definition from the list on the right. Compare your choices with a classmate's and make corrections if necessary.

Words		Definitions/Synonyms
1. prison	**a.**	keep safe
2. disgrace	**b.**	someone who has to stay in jail
3. so-called	**c.**	a person's actions
4. behavior	**d.**	metal pieces on windows and doors of jails
5. commit	**e.**	jail
6. prisoner	**f.**	make someone better
7. criminals	**g.**	get away from
8. authorities	**h.**	considered as
9. reform	**i.**	people who are bosses or officials
10. naive	**j.**	thieves, robbers, killers
11. security	**k.**	safety
12. escape	**l.**	simple; childish
13. bars	**m.**	do or perform
14. protect	**n.**	strong and dangerous
15. violent	**o.**	something to be ashamed of

19 Writing

Think about something that makes you very angry. Some ideas are: dangerous drivers, unfair teachers or bosses, cruelty to animals, dirty cities. Talk about these ideas with two or three classmates, and then choose one idea. Write a letter to the editor of a newspaper. Include these things in your letter:

- Say why you are angry.
- Give at least three examples of the problem that makes you angry.
- Suggest a solution.

After writing your first draft, read it to a classmate, and ask for suggestions. Revise your draft.

20 Final Activity

Look at your local newspaper. Choose three stories and write new headlines in English. Exchange papers with a classmate. *Without looking at the newspaper*, write a short paragraph for each of your classmate's headlines. Then sit in groups of three or four. Read your headlines and stories aloud to your group.

UNIT 6

COMMUNICATION
Talking about a visit to the dentist •
Listening to and talking about problems,
and giving advice • Giving reasons •
Talking about frequency of activities

GRAMMAR
Inseparable two-word verbs • Statements
with *because* • Position of adverbs of
frequency

SKILLS
Reading an interview • Writing
advice for different problems

At the Dentist's Office

Bob and Lisa Logan are at the dentist's for a checkup.

LISA: I'm nervous! I want to go home!

BOB: Just relax, Lisa. This is only a checkup. You don't have a toothache, so there's nothing to be nervous about. Dr. Warren is just going to look at your teeth today.

LISA: You told me that last year, and he had to pull one of my teeth.

BOB: But last year you ate a lot of candy and cake, and you never took care of your teeth. This year you're brushing after every meal, right?

LISA: Yeah. But maybe I have some cavities anyway.

BOB: Then Dr. Warren will fill them another day. It doesn't hurt. I wish you wouldn't complain so much.

DR. WARREN: OK. Who's going to be the first patient?

BOB: Why don't you take care of Lisa first?

LISA: Well, thanks a lot! Are you sure you aren't nervous about *your* checkup?

DR. WARREN: Come in and sit down, Lisa. I just want to clean your teeth today, and look at them. I'll check your gums, too. There's no need to be afraid.

1 Vocabulary in Context 🔲

Talking about a visit to the dentist

Complete each sentence with the correct word or expression.

brush	complain	patient
cavities	dentist	pull
checkup	gums	take care of
clean	hurt	toothache

Dr. Warren is Bob and Lisa's (1) _____ . Last year Lisa didn't
(2) _____ her teeth. Sometimes she didn't remember to
(3) _____ them. One day Lisa had a very bad
(4) _____ , and Dr. Warren had to (5) _____ her
tooth. Now Lisa is afraid to see the dentist because she's afraid it will
(6) _____ . Bob doesn't want Lisa to (7) _____ , but he
doesn't want to be the first (8) _____ , either. Both Lisa and Bob
are nervous about their (9) _____; but Dr. Warren only wants to
(10) _____ their teeth, and check their teeth for
(11) _____ . He wants to check their (12) _____ , too.

2 Presentation 🔲

Inseparable two-word verbs

> Some two-word verbs cannot be separated:
> **come in, come back, look at, look for, sit down.**

1. **Come in** to my office, Lisa.

2. I want to **look at** your teeth.

3. I have to **look for** cavities.

4. Please **sit down** in this chair.

5. Oh dear, you'll have to **come back** in two weeks so I can fill
   your cavities.

3 Practice

Complete the following conversation using one of the two-word verbs from *2*.

DR. WARREN: Well, Bob, it's your turn now. Please (1) _____ . It's getting late, so I just have time to (2) _____ your teeth today.

BOB: Uh — Dr. Warren, you don't have to (3) _____ my teeth today. I can (4) _____ another day.

DR. WARREN: No, no. That's OK. Just (5) _____ and relax. I'm just going to (6) _____ cavities or other problems.

BOB: Other problems? Uh . . . Gosh, Dr. Warren, I don't feel very well. I've got a bad headache . . .

DR. WARREN: Look, Bob, just (7) _____ now and (8) _____ in this chair. I'm not going to hurt you!

BOB: Well, OK. But what other problems are you going to (9) _____ ?

DR. WARREN: Oh, I have to check your gums, you know. I want to see if you are taking good care of your teeth. Then when you (10) _____ next week, we'll clean your teeth.

4 Interaction

Work with a partner. Pretend you just went to the dentist. Then exchange roles.

A: I went to see my dentist the other day.

B: Oh, what did | he / she | say?

A: | He / She | told me to _____ .

B: Did | he / she | have to _____ ?

A: _____ .

5 Reentry

Read each of the problems below. Then give advice using *should* and *shouldn't*. Use the phrases in the advice box to make sentences, or make up your own sentences.

> Bob has to study.
>
> He shouldn't go swimming.

> Liz wants a new job.
>
> She should check the ads in the newspaper.

Problems	Advice
1. Sam has a toothache.	go to driving school
2. My car won't start.	become a secretary
3. Gloria has an exam tomorrow.	go to the dentist
4. Ted's sick today.	shop at the department store
5. Cristina can't drive.	eat a lot of sugar
6. I don't like to type.	go swimming
7. I have to buy some clothes and gifts.	find a good mechanic
8. Cristina and Gino need exercise.	stay in bed and rest
9. Sekila has a bad earache.	watch TV
10. Lisa has a lot of cavities.	

6 Presentation

Giving reasons

> Use **because** to give the reason or cause of something.

1. Lisa had problems with her teeth **because** she didn't take care of them.

2. Gino's happy **because** he doesn't have any cavities.

3. Liz is unhappy **because** she doesn't like her job.

Practice

Make sentences with *because* using one sentence from the first column and one from the second column. Use each sentence only once. The first one is done for you.

> Lisa had a lot of cavities because she didn't take care of her teeth.

1.	Lisa had a lot of cavities.	**a.**	It used too much gas.
2.	Gloria isn't at school today.	**b.**	He has to study.
3.	Ted wants a calculator.	**c.**	They played well.
4.	Lisa and Joyce walk to school.	**d.**	She wasn't feeling well.
5.	Mike plays soccer.	**e.**	The building was on fire.
6.	Bob went to the dentist.	**f.**	He didn't do the homework.
7.	The Tigers won yesterday.	**g.**	He had a toothache.
8.	Tom sold his big car.	**h.**	They didn't want to cook.
9.	The Youngs ate in a restaurant last night.	**i.**	She was nervous about her checkup.
10.	Sekila went to the doctor.	**j.**	He likes to do math problems quickly.
11.	I left the party early.	**k.**	It was boring.
12.	He jumped from the window.	**l.**	She didn't take care of her teeth.
13.	Sam can't go to the movies.	**m.**	He likes it and it's good exercise.
14.	Lisa was complaining.	**n.**	It's close to their homes.
15.	Ted can't answer the question.	**o.**	She's sick.

8 **Practice**

Work with a partner. Ask and answer questions about each sentence in the first column in *7*. You can make up your own answers.

> A: Why did Lisa have a lot of cavities?
> B: Because she ate a lot of candy.

9 Interaction

Complete each question. Then sit with three classmates. Take turns asking questions and giving answers. Use your imagination if necessary.

> A: Why did you go ___to the dentist's___ yesterday?
> B: | Because ___I had a bad toothache___ .
> | To ___have her look at my teeth___ .

1. Why did you go _____ yesterday?
2. Why are you _____ ?
3. Why do you _____ every day?
4. Why were you _____ last week?
5. Why didn't you call _____ yesterday?
6. Why do you want _____ ?
7. Why are you buying _____ ?
8. Why did you complain to _____ yesterday?

10 Presentation

Position of adverbs of frequency

> The position of adverbs of frequency depends on the verb.
> (Remember: Adverbs of frequency go *before* main verbs. See page 57.)
>
> 1. In sentences with **be**: subject + **be** + adverb
>
>   He's **rarely** sick.
>
> 2. In sentences with an auxiliary verb:
>   subject + auxiliary verb + adverb + verb
>
>   He will **never** finish his homework.
>   I can **usually** tell when she's angry.
>
> 3. To ask **do** questions: **do** + subject + adverb + verb
>
>   Do you **always** brush your teeth after every meal?

A
> A: Does Bob **often** have cavities?
> B: No. He **rarely** has cavities because he **always** brushes his teeth.

B
> A: Do Bob and Lisa **always** brush their teeth?
> B: Yes. They are **usually** careful to brush after every meal.

11 Practice

Make a sentence using the adverbs of frequency.

> Tom Logan is in his office from 8:30 AM to 5:30 PM. / always
>
> Tom Logan is always in his office from 8:30 AM to 5:30 PM.

> Does Sekila go to a lot of parties? / rarely
>
> No, she rarely goes to parties.

1. Sam is at home on Sundays. / usually
2. Does Sam go to school after work? / sometimes
3. Liz will help her family. / always
4. Ted can remember his homework. / usually
5. Does Gloria tell Sekila her problems? / rarely
6. Cristina will telephone Gino on Sundays. / often
7. Adela is angry with her children. / never
8. Do Cristina and Gino have arguments? / sometimes
9. Sam can see his girlfriend on weekends. / usually
10. Elinor is bored with her patients. / never

12 Practice

Work with a partner. Ask and answer questions about Liz's employment record at the telephone company.

> A: Does Liz work hard?
> B: Yes, she usually works hard.

EMPLOYMENT RECORD				
ELIZABETH YOUNG	10 South Kennedy Ave.		Winfield, New York 11500	
	Always	**Usually**	**Rarely**	**Never**
Arrives late				X
Is polite	X			
Misses work			X	
Understands directions	X			
Learns fast		X		
Works hard		X		
Is careless				X
Answers questions well	X			
Will work extra hours		X		

Reentry

If-clauses with present tense verbs, *can*, and *should*

A. **Tell what usually happens using one phrase from the first box and one from the second.**

If Nancy has a toothache, she goes to the dentist.

1. If I have a cold,	they put an ad in the paper.
2. If Warner's Department Store has a sale,	I make a cake.
	she can't study.
3. If somebody has a birthday,	he takes his friends to lunch.
4. If Sekila's nervous,	I go to bed early.
5. If Mike has a lot of money,	

B. **Now tell what's possible using one phrase from the first box and one from the second.**

1. If Adela graduates with good grades,	we can have dinner in the yard.
2. If Cristina gets married in October,	you can get a job as an international flight attendant.
3. If it doesn't rain,	her mother can come to the wedding.
4. If you can speak a foreign language,	she can get a good job.

C. **Give advice using one phrase from the first box and one from the second.**

1. If you want to be a good athlete,	you should try Mario's Restaurant.
2. If you like Italian food,	you shouldn't eat too much or stay out late.
3. If you want to have a good time,	you shouldn't eat a lot of sugar.
4. If you don't want to get cavities,	you should go to Rio on your vacation.

14 Interaction

Work with a partner. Take turns asking for and giving advice.

> A: I want to _____ .
> B: Then you | should | _____ .
> | shouldn't

15 Listening

First Listening

Number your paper from 1-5. Read each problem. Then listen to each conversation and write the letter of the problem.

Problems:

a. The speaker's daughter isn't doing very well in school.
b. One of the speaker's friends doesn't talk to him anymore, and he feels terrible about it.
c. The speaker wants to get married, but her parents don't like her boyfriend.
d. The speaker can't find a job.
e. The speaker needs a vacation.

Second Listening

Now number your paper from 1-20. Listen to the conversations again, and write *T* (True), *F* (False), or *NG* (Not Given) for each statement.

Conversation 1

  1. Dave is looking for a job.
  2. Bill went to an employment agency.
  3. Dave does not have a job now.
  4. Dave does not read the help wanted ads.

Conversation 2

  5. It's summer vacation.
  6. Martha's daughter can't hear.
  7. Martha's daughter reads well.
  8. Martha is very proud of her daughter.

Conversation 3

9. Steve is giving Rita some advice.
10. Steve knows what the problem is.
11. Rita is going to talk to Steve's friend.
12. Steve is going to talk to his friend.

Conversation 4

13. Tanya wants to marry Peter.
14. Tanya talked to her parents about the situation.
15. Tanya's parents want to hurt her.
16. Joan tells Tanya to talk to her parents.

Conversation 5

17. The dentist is worried about his patients.
18. Dr. Erickson will go on vacation.
19. The dentist's wife is worried about her husband.
20. The dentist wants to spend some time with his wife.

16 Writing

Read each problem, then write a short paragraph giving advice. Read your paragraphs to one or two classmates. Ask for suggestions. Then revise your paragraphs.

> **Problem:** Bob Logan's schoolwork isn't as good this year as it was last year. This year he's working part-time, and he goes out a lot with his friends.
>
> **Advice:** Bob should spend more time on his homework, because that will help him do better at school. He shouldn't go out during the week, because it makes him too tired for school. He should see his friends only on weekends. Maybe he should work fewer hours at his job.

Problem 1: Gino and Cristina are going to get married. They don't have a lot of money. They want a small wedding, but they both have big families and a lot of friends.

Problem 2: Mike Young can't decide what to do after he graduates from high school. His father is an engineer, and he wants Mike to be an engineer, too. Mike likes to study languages, and he wants to travel.

Problem 3: Tom Logan has to work very hard. He's at the travel agency all day and sometimes at night, too. He doesn't have time to eat good food and he looks really thin.

Problem 4: Sekila Manzikala wants to go home to Zaire for her vacation, but she doesn't have a lot of money. She will finish college in one year.

17 Reading

Before You Read

1. What does a dentist do?
2. Would you like to be a dentist? Why or why not?
3. Why do you think that some people want to be dentists?

First Reading

Read the questions below before reading "An Interview with Dr. Caplan." Think about the questions as you read. Then, write the answers to the questions.

1. What two things must you do to take care of your teeth and mouth?
2. Name five reasons someone might become a dentist.
3. How many employees do most dentists have? What do they do?
4. Who takes care of the patients when the dentist goes on vacation?

AN INTERVIEW WITH DR. CAPLAN

Dr. Carl M. Caplan is Associate Dean for Clinical Affairs of the Dental School at Georgetown University. He helps train new dentists.

INTERCOM 2000: Thank you for talking with us, Dr. Caplan. Tell me, why does someone decide to become a dentist?

DR. CAPLAN: People become dentists for several reasons. Usually, they like to help people, and they like working with their hands. A dentist can be his or her own boss. Also, a dentist can make a good living for his or her family. And a good dentist is respected by the community.

INTERCOM 2000: Do dentists worry about preventing cavities?

DR. CAPLAN: Oh yes, prevention is very important. Dentists tell their patients to take care of their teeth and mouths by eating healthy food and brushing their teeth. That way, they won't have as many cavities or other tooth or gum problems.

INTERCOM 2000: Does anyone help dentists with their patients?

DR. CAPLAN: Yes, most dentists employ a receptionist who greets patients and makes appointments, a chairside assistant who helps the dentist with patients, and a dental hygienist who cleans patients' teeth.

INTERCOM 2000: Dentists must be very busy. Can they ever take a vacation?

DR. CAPLAN: Everybody knows you have to take care of yourself if you're going to try to take care of someone else. Most dentists I know try to take a vacation every year. When they do, they always ask another dentist to cover for them. Someone must always be available to take care of dental patients. After all, emergencies do happen!

INTERCOM 2000: Thank you again, Dr. Caplan. This has been very interesting.

Second Reading

Reread the interview with Dr. Caplan. Write down three things that are good about being a dentist. Write your own ideas of three things you would not like about being a dentist. Share your ideas with a classmate.

18 Final Activity

Work with a partner, and role play a visit to the dentist.

A parent is taking his/her child to the dentist. The child will not let the dentist examine his/her mouth. The dentist tries to convince the child *why* it's important to examine his/her teeth. The child still refuses. The parent tries to convince the child. The child refuses again. The parent promises a nice surprise for the child. The child still keeps his/her mouth closed. What happens next? Who wins?

> **Useful words and phrases:**
>
> Please open wide.
> I need to look at your teeth.
> I'm not going to hurt you.
> This is just a checkup.
> It's very important to take care of your teeth and gums.

After you practice, perform your conversation for the class.

<table>
<tr>
<td>

UNIT
7

</td>
<td>

COMMUNICATION
Talking about weight and health problems ▪
Giving excuses or reasons ▪ Talking about
future conditions

</td>
<td>

GRAMMAR
Prepositions of time: *in* and *for* ▪ *Too +
adjective + to +* verb ▪ *Every, every other* ▪
Future conditional clauses with *if* ▪ *All of, some
of, none of* ▪ *Too* + adjective + *for* + object

SKILLS
Reading about exercise ▪ Giving information to
a doctor

</td>
</tr>
</table>

A Weight Problem?

Cristina is at Dr. Young's office for a checkup.

DR. YOUNG: What seems to be the problem,
                Cristina?

CRISTINA: I'm not sure. I'm very tired and
                I look awful. I think I need to
                lose weight. I want to be in good
                shape for my wedding.

DR. YOUNG: Hmm. You have a small frame and your height is five feet, four
                inches. You should weigh between 114 and 127 pounds.
                Your weight is 115 pounds. You're certainly not too heavy for
                your height!

CRISTINA: But I *feel* heavy. I don't have any energy. I'm too tired to do
                anything.

DR. YOUNG: Tell me about your diet. What do you eat for breakfast?

CRISTINA: Oh, I just have a cup of coffee. I don't want to get fat.

DR. YOUNG: You're not fat, and you need a good breakfast! What about
                exercise? You should exercise every day.

CRISTINA: But I work all day, and I'm too tired to exercise after work.

DR. YOUNG: Look, Cristina, if you exercise a little every day you'll look and
                feel better. If you eat a good breakfast, you'll have more energy.

CRISTINA: Well, OK. If I get up earlier, I'll have time for breakfast. Maybe
                I can walk to work every day and play tennis every other day.
                That'll be good exercise.

Unit Seven   77

Gino is also having a checkup. He says he's too tired to play basketball or go out at night.

DR. YOUNG: Of course you're too tired to
play basketball or go out at night!
Look at this chart. You have a medium frame and you're five
nine. You should weigh between 148 and 160 pounds, but you
weigh 170. You're too heavy!

GINO: Well, I *did* gain a lot of weight this year, but . . .

DR. YOUNG: Look, Gino, I'm going to put you on a diet. Follow it for six
weeks, then come back and see me.

GINO: OK, I guess you're right. And I do want to be in good shape for
my wedding. I'll come back and see you in six weeks.

HEIGHT AND WEIGHT CHART							
MEN				WOMEN			
Height ft. in.	Small frame	Medium frame	Large frame	Height ft. in.	Small frame	Medium frame	Large frame
5' 4"	132-138	135-145	142-156	5' 0"	104-115	113-126	122-137
5' 5"	134-140	137-148	144-160	5' 1"	106-118	115-129	125-140
5' 6"	136-142	139-151	146-164	5' 2"	108-121	118-132	128-143
5' 7"	138-145	142-154	149-168	5' 3"	111-124	121-135	131-147
5' 8"	140-148	145-157	152-172	5' 4"	114-127	124-138	134-151
5' 9"	142-151	148-160	155-176	5' 5"	117-130	127-141	137-155
5' 10"	144-154	151-163	158-180	5' 6"	120-133	130-144	140-159
5' 11"	146-157	154-166	161-184	5' 7"	123-136	133-147	143-163
6' 0"	149-160	157-170	164-188	5' 8"	126-139	136-150	146-167
6' 1"	152-164	160-174	168-192	5' 9"	129-142	139-153	149-170

1 Vocabulary in Context

Talking about weight

Complete the conversation with these words and expressions. Change the form if necessary, and use each item only once.

diet	gain weight	height	on a diet
fat	healthy	how tall	weigh
follow	heavy	lose weight	weight
frame			

DR. YOUNG: (1) _____ are you, Susan?
SUSAN: I'm five six.
DR. YOUNG: How much do you (2) _____ ?
SUSAN: One hundred twenty-five pounds. I want to (3) _____ , so I'm on a diet.
DR. YOUNG: But 125 pounds is a good (4) _____ for you. You have a medium (5) _____ . You're not too (6) _____ for your (7) _____ . You're very (8) _____ . You don't have to (9) _____ .

* * *

DR. YOUNG: How much do you weigh, Linda?
LINDA: A hundred and sixty pounds. I was nervous last year and I ate a lot, so I (10) _____ . And now I'm really (11) _____ !
DR. YOUNG: Well, you *do* need to lose some weight. I'm going to put you (12) _____ . (13) _____ the diet for a month and come back and see me.

2 Practice

Look at the heights, frames, and weights of these people. According to the chart on page 78, who is or isn't too heavy? Who should go on a diet? Who doesn't have to lose weight? Use the units of measure that are used where you live.

Jim / 5'10" (1.77 m) / small / 170 lb (77 kg)
A: Jim is five feet, ten inches tall. He has a small frame and he weighs 170 pounds.
B: He's too heavy. He should go on a diet.

> Sylvia / 5'6" (1.67 m) / large / 135 lb (61 kg)
> A: Sylvia is five feet, six inches tall. She has a large frame, and she weighs 135 pounds.
> B: She isn't too heavy. She doesn't have to lose weight.

1. Steven / 5'8" (1.72 m) / medium / 172 lb (78 kg)
2. Juan / 5'6" (1.67 m) / large / 157 lb (71 kg)
3. Alexa / 5'2" (1.57 m) / small / 134 lb (61 kg)
4. Helen / 5'7" (1.70 m) / medium / 148 lb (67 kg)
5. Tom / 6'1" (1.85 m) / medium / 172 lb (78 kg)
6. Maria / 5'3" (1.60 m) / large / 141 lb (64 kg)
7. Joe / 5'9" (1.75 m) / medium / 150 lb (68 kg)
8. Sue / 5'8" (1.72 m) / small / 147 lb (67 kg)
9. Diana / 5'4" (1.62 m) / medium / 137 lb (63 kg)
10. Erik / 5'11" (1.80 m) / small / 157 lb (71 kg)

3 Presentation

Prepositions of time: *in* and *for*

> Use **in** to mean "after a period of time."
> Use **for** to show continuous action for a period of time.

1. Gino Leone has to be on a diet **for** six weeks.
2. He's going to see Dr. Young again **in** six weeks.

4 Practice

Complete the sentences with *in* or *for*.

> Gino called Cristina, but her phone was busy. He's going to call again ___*in*___ an hour.
>
> Mike is studying at the library. He's going to be there ___*for*___ three hours.

1. I'm going to go to the movies _____ ten minutes.
2. Mike studied Spanish _____ a year.

3. He was in Mexico _____ two months last year.
4. My aunt is sixty-four years old. She's going to retire _____ a year.
5. Ted was sick last month. He didn't go to school _____ a week.
6. I visited my uncle in the hospital. I'm going to see him again _____ two or three days.
7. Gino and Cristina are going to be married _____ two months.
8. Martha is walking quickly. She has to be at work _____ three minutes.
9. Bill isn't finished. He needs to work _____ ten more minutes.
10. That TV show is long. It's on _____ three hours.

5 Reentry

Prepositions

Complete the paragraph with *at, for, in, on, to,* or *until*.

Elinor Young usually walks (1) _____ her office (2) _____ the morning. It's (3) _____ Prince Street, not far from her house. There are often patients (4) _____ the waiting room when she arrives. Dr. Young sees her first patient (5) _____ 9:00. She usually takes a half hour (6) _____ lunch and works (7) _____ 3:00. Then she goes (8) _____ Winfield Hospital (9) _____ Main Street to visit her patients there. On Friday she works (10) _____ the hospital all day. She often works (11) _____ Saturday or Sunday.

6 Vocabulary in Context

More adjectives

1. Some foods are **fattening**. If you eat a lot of these foods, you will gain weight.
2. That's a **violent** neighborhood — there are crimes there every day.
3. That music is much too **loud**. It hurts my ears.
4. I feel **lazy** today. I don't want to do any work.

Work with a partner to ask and answer questions. Say *no* and give an excuse or a reason with *too*. Choose your answers from the adjectives in the box — or make up your own!

> A: Did Liz finish reading that magazine?
> B: No, she was too busy.

sick	expensive	difficult
boring	lazy	busy
fattening	tired	upset
violent	loud	heavy

1. Does Gino look good in his new suit?

2. Do you want to go to the party?

3. Did you finish your homework?

4. Will you be in class the next time?

5. Did you enjoy the last movie you saw?

6. Do you like hamburgers?

7. Do you want to go to that new restaurant with us?

8. Are you cooking dinner tonight?

9. Do you play tennis?

10. Are you going to go grocery shopping tomorrow?

8 **Presentation**

Giving excuses or reasons

> Use **too** + *adjective* + **to** + *verb* to give an excuse or reason why an activity cannot be done.

1. Cristina's very tired. Cristina can't go running.
    Cristina's **too tired to go** running.

2. I'm very busy. I can't go to the movies.
    I'm **too busy to go** to the movies.

9 Practice

Work with a partner. Take turns role playing each student. Student A tells about a problem. Student B gives a possible reason or excuse for the problem. Use:

> **maybe** . . . **too** + adjective + **to** + verb

Choose a problem from the Box 1 or talk about a real problem. Use an adjective from Box 2, or choose a different adjective.

> A: My boyfriend doesn't take me to nice restaurants.
> B: Maybe he's too broke to take you to nice restaurants.

Box 1: Problems
doesn't answer the phone
doesn't send me flowers
doesn't write letters
doesn't help with the dishes
doesn't cook very well
doesn't answer my questions
doesn't get to school on time
doesn't listen to his/her parents
doesn't love me

Box 2: Adjectives	
broke	nervous
busy	selfish
lazy	tired

Useful vocabulary:

be broke = not have any money

10 Presentation

Every, every other

> Use singular nouns after **every** and **every other**.

A

Sunday	Monday	Tuesday	Wednesday	Thursday	Friday	Saturday
Walked 3 miles	Walked 3 miles	Walked 3 miles	Walked 3 miles	Walked 3 miles	Walked 3 miles	Walked 3 miles

Last week Gino walked three miles **every day**.

B

Sunday	Monday	Tuesday	Wednesday	Thursday	Friday	Saturday
Played Tennis		Played Tennis		Played Tennis		Played Tennis

Last week Cristina played tennis **every other day**.

11 Practice

Work with a partner. Take turns asking and giving information.

> A: Name every year from 1970 to 1980.
> B: 1970, 1971, 1972, 1973, 1974, 1975, 1976, 1977, 1978, 1979, 1980.
> A: Name every other year from 1950 to 1960.
> B: 1950, 1952, 1954, 1956, 1958, 1960.

1. Name every month.
2. Name every other month.
3. Name every day of the week.
4. Say every other number from 100 to 80.
5. Say every other letter of the alphabet.
6. Name every TV show you watched last night.
7. Name every movie you went to last month.
8. Name every English teacher you know.

12 Presentation

Future conditional clauses with *if*

> After an *if*-clause, use **will** to express a future condition.

1. If you don't eat breakfast, you'll feel tired.
2. If you don't exercise regularly, you won't get in better shape.

13 Practice

Make sentences that tell about a future condition.

> Gino / eat a lot of pizza / get fat
> If Gino eats a lot of pizza, he'll get fat.
>
> Cristina / drink too much coffee / sleep well
> If Cristina drinks too much coffee, she won't sleep well.

1. Gino / eat a lot of vegetables / lose weight

2. Cristina / get more exercise / feel better

3. Joyce / stay in bed late / be late to school

4. Dr. Young / not listen to her patients / understand their problems

5. Tom / works every weekend / have fun with his family

6. Mike / not do homework / get good grades in school

7. Sekila / write home every week / make her parents happy

8. Cristina and Gino / spend a lot of money / be able to buy an apartment

9. Adela / get too tired / be able to help Lisa with homework

10. Howard / eat breakfast / feel hungry before lunch

14 Practice

A friend is going to begin studying English. Write five sentences telling him/her what to do and what *not* to do. Use *If . . . , you will . . .*

> If you look up every new word in your dictionary, you will spend an hour reading one paragraph.

Sit with two or three classmates. Take turns reading your sentences. Choose the five sentences that give the most useful ideas for studying English. Share your group's sentences with the rest of the class.

15 Presentation

All (of), some of, none of

> **All (of), some of, none of** are followed by:
> • a plural noun,
> • a pronoun, *or*
> • a noncountable noun.

1. They're having a party. They're inviting | **all** | their **friends.**
                                            | **all of** |

2. We're having a small wedding. We're inviting **some of** our **friends.**

3. The Logans aren't on diets. **None of them** need to lose weight.

4. Ted can watch TV. He did | **all** | his **homework**.
                            | **all of** |

5. Joyce can't watch TV. She did **some** of her **homework**, but she didn't finish it.

16 Practice

Work in groups of three or four. Describe the pictures using *all of, some of,* and *none of.* Write the group's descriptions, and share it with the class.

There are several students in the cafeteria. Some of the students are eating and some of them are studying. None of them are dancing.

1.

There are several people at the swimming pool. . . .

2.

There are several people in the park. . . .

3.

There are several people at the concert. . . .

4.

There are several mechanics at the garage. . . .

5.

There are several people at the party. . . .

17 Listening

Listen to the phone conversation. Write the day, the date, and the time of each patient's appointment. Also check the reason for the visit.

APPOINTMENTS			
Patient's Name	Day and Date	Time	Reasons for Visit
Howard Young			☐ checkup ☐ fill cavity ☐ cleaning ☐ pull tooth
Joyce Young			☐ checkup ☐ fill cavity ☐ cleaning ☐ pull tooth
Ted Young			☐ checkup ☐ fill cavity ☐ cleaning ☐ pull tooth
Elinor Young			☐ checkup ☐ fill cavity ☐ cleaning ☐ pull tooth

18 Presentation

***Too* + adjective + *for* + object**

1. It's very windy. We can't play tennis.
   It's **too windy for us** to play tennis.
2. It's very late. The children can't go outside.
   It's **too late for the children** to go outside.

19 Practice

Work with a partner. Agree with the statements, using *too...for*.

> A: Sam can't go skiing because it's very warm.
> B: You're right. It's too warm for him to go skiing.

1. We won't watch the races because it's very cold.
2. Pablo and Melanie can't play tennis because it's very windy.
3. Ana can't go to the movies because it's very late.
4. Mike can't run because it's very hot.
5. You can't take a picture because it's very cloudy.
6. I can't cook Chinese food well because it's very difficult.
7. Beth can't study here because it's very noisy.
8. Phil can't find his keys because it's very dark.

20 Reentry

Questions with *how often*: adverbs of frequency

Complete the first column in the chart, using frequency adverbs (*never, rarely, sometimes, often*) to show how often you do the activity. Then interview two classmates. Write their names at the top of the next two columns. Ask them how often they do each activity and write the adverb of frequency for each activity.

Activity	Me		
1. Watch television			
2. Go to the movies			
3. Go to museums			
4. Play sports			
5. Read books			

Now make sentences about your activities and your classmates' activities.

A: How often do you ____*watch television*____ ?
B: ____*I rarely watch television*____ .

21 Reading

Before You Read

1. Do you exercise regularly?
2. What facts do you know about the benefits of exercise?
3. Do you know which sports use the most calories?

First Reading

Sit in groups of three or four. Discuss the questions in "Before You Read." Then scan (look rapidly through) the information in the article on exercise. Work together to find the words and expressions listed below and to use the context to guess what they mean. Write down the meanings your group decides on. Then check with your teacher or the dictionary.

1. myth
2. premature
3. reap benefits
4. sedentary
5. consumed

Myth: No pain, no gain.
Fact: You don't have to hurt to be fit. Moderate exercise improves the working of the lungs and heart, may reduce the risk of premature death — and is relatively pain-free. In fact, if you feel pain, not just discomfort, you should slow down or stop or you will injure yourself.

Myth: I need to exercise for 45 minutes or more to do any good.
Fact: Breaking a sweat for 20 to 30 minutes three or four times a week is enough to reap major health benefits. More than this will make you fitter — but not necessarily healthier. And finding an hour for exercise is impractical for many people and unnecessary for most.

Myth: I can get in shape exercising 10 to 15 minutes once or twice a week.
Fact: That's not much better than nothing. But new studies do show that 15 minutes or more three to four days a week does do some good, especially for previously sedentary people.

Myth: If I stop exercising for a short time, I'll lose everything and have to start over again.

Fact: Staying in shape is easier than getting fit in the first place. After you reach a level of fitness, even taking a week off to rest a minor injury won't put you back to the beginning. A longer rest will make a difference, so if an injury stops you from working out normally, try changing to another activity. Swimming, for example, is a good way to stay in shape while resting a sore knee.

Myth: Women who lift weights get big muscles.
Fact: Women can increase strength and endurance without building bulky muscles, because they have far less testosterone — a hormone necessary for building muscles — than men do. For women to develop larger muscles through weight lifting requires an intensive training program.

Myth: Exercising will make me eat more.
Fact: Your appetite may increase in response to an intense, vigorous exercise program, but a moderate one won't have much effect. And exercising just before you eat will make you less hungry. Raising your body temperature through exercise decreases your appetite.

Fitness Facts

Time needed to burn the calories consumed in—	Bag of potato chips (150 calories)	Chocolate bar (270 calories)	Bagel and cream cheese (574 calories)	Pancakes with syrup, butter and bacon (849 calories)
Running	13 min.	23 min.	48 min.	1 hr. 11 min.
Bicycling	14 min.	25 min.	52 min.	1 hr. 17 min.
Walking	21 min.	39 min.	1 hr. 22 min	2 hr. 1 min.
Aerobics	25 min.	45 min.	1 hr. 36 min.	2 hr. 22 min.
Swimming	30 min.	54 min.	1 hr. 55 min.	2 hr. 50 min.
Golf	38 min.	1 hr. 8 min.	2 hr. 24 min.	3 hr. 32 min.
Bowling	50 min.	1 hr. 30 min.	3 hr. 11 min.	4 hr. 43 min.

Second Reading

Read the article again and consult the chart. Work by yourself to find the correct answers to the following questions.

1. "No pain, no gain" means that if you
   a. don't hurt while you exercise, you won't get fat.
   b. don't hurt while you exercise, you won't get fit.
   c. don't hurt while you exercise, you will gain weight.

2. If you break a sweat,
   a. you must fix it.
   b. you are exercising hard enough to perspire.
   c. your sweatshirt and sweatpants don't match.

3. To get in shape you should exercise
   a. 3 or 4 times a week.
   b. 10 to 15 minutes once or twice a week.
   c. for 45 minutes every day.

4. If you get injured you should
   a. stop exercising.
   b. choose a different way to exercise.
   c. start over from the beginning slowly and gently.

5. Exercising just before you eat will
   a. make you eat the same amount.
   b. make you eat more.
   c. make you eat less.

6. To burn the 574 calories of a bagel with cream cheese, you must
   a. run for 52 minutes.
   b. bowl for 3 years and 11 days.
   c. swim for 1 hour and 55 minutes.

7. According to the chart, the quickest way to burn calories is by
   a. doing aerobics.
   b. walking.
   c. running.

8. From looking at the chart you can tell that
   a. aerobics is the best exercise for everyone.
   b. some exercises burn more calories than others.
   c. foods that have more calories taste better.

22 Writing

Pretend that you are waiting to see the doctor. The receptionist gives you a form to complete. Fill in the form. (You do not have to tell the truth!)

PATIENT INFORMATION FORM

Name _____   Date _____

Address _____   Phone _____

_____

Height _____   Weight _____   Age _____

What is your present physical condition? (Check one)

____ poor ____ fair ____ good ____ excellent

What exercise(s) do you do? _____

_____

How frequently? _____

Describe your diet for the last three days: _____

_____

_____

_____

_____

How many hours do you usually sleep each night? _____

Is your sleep restful? _____

Do you have any of the following conditions? If so, describe.

    • Too tired _____

    • Too nervous _____

    • Too heavy _____

    • Too thin _____

Why do you need medical advice at this time? _____

_____

_____

Final Activity

Work with a classmate. One person is the doctor and one is the patient. Use the information that you wrote in *22* (Patient Information Form.) The doctor reads the information and gives advice about any problems. Here is a model.

DOCTOR: You sleep only four hours a night. You should sleep more.
PATIENT: I can't. I have a lot of work.
DOCTOR: Why don't you go to bed an hour earlier?
PATIENT: I should, but I like to watch the news.
DOCTOR: But you need more sleep. If you don't sleep enough,
          you will get sick.
PATIENT: OK, I'll try to sleep more.

COMMUNICATION
Talking about table items ▪ Talking about diets ▪ Offering, accepting, and refusing food ▪ Ordering and taking orders in a restaurant

GRAMMAR
Even + adjective ▪ Comparative adjectives with spelling changes ▪ Contrast of *some*

and *any* ▪ Irregular past tense: *begin, lose, feel, sleep* ▪ Contrast between *some* + noncountable noun and quantity + noncountable noun

SKILLS
Reading about a diet plan ▪ Filling out an application

On a Diet

Dr. Young gives Gino a diet to help him lose weight.

DR. YOUNG: Here's your diet, Gino. Remember to follow it carefully.

GINO: Is this all I can eat? One small glass of juice, one hard-boiled egg . . . That isn't enough! I'm going to be hungry all day! Can't I have fried eggs?

DR. YOUNG: I'm sorry, Gino. Not when you're on the diet.

GINO: Can't I even eat bread?

DR. YOUNG: You can have some bread, but you can't have any butter.

GINO: What about pizza and spaghetti?

DR. YOUNG: No pizza and no spaghetti.

GINO: But I cook pizza and spaghetti every day at the Roma!

DR. YOUNG: Sorry, Gino. Look at it this way — if you lose weight, you will feel better, look better, and have more energy. *And* you'll be in better shape for your wedding!

Here is the diet plan Dr. Young gave Gino.

Daily Meal Plan

Choose one breakfast

Small glass of tomato juice
Hard- or soft-boiled egg
Thin slice of toast (without butter)
Cup of tea or coffee (with low-fat milk, no sugar)

or
Small glass of pineapple juice
Thin slice of toast (without butter)
Slice of low-fat cheese
Cup of tea or coffee (with low-fat milk, no sugar)

or
Small glass of grapefruit juice
Bowl of cereal with skim milk
Cup of tea or coffee (with low-fat milk, no sugar)

Choose one lunch

Low-fat yogurt with fruit
Lettuce & tomato salad
Slice of whole-wheat
   bread
Glass of skim milk

or

Bowl of chicken soup
Tuna salad (made with
   low-fat yogurt)
Slice of whole-wheat
   bread
Half a grapefruit
Glass of skim milk

or

Two slices of turkey
Slice of whole-wheat
   bread
Grapes
Glass of skim milk

Choose one dinner

Glass of tomato juice
Small broiled steak (no fat)
Tossed salad: lettuce,
   tomatoes, green
   peppers, and celery
Asparagus
Baked potato (plain)
Small apple
Cup of herbal tea

or

Glass of tomato juice
Small piece of broiled fish
Tossed salad
Broccoli
Slice of whole wheat
   bread (no butter)
Small pear
Cup of herbal tea

or

Glass of tomato juice
Small piece of baked
   chicken (no skin or fat)
Tossed salad
Green beans
Baked potato (plain)
Cup of fruit salad
Cup of herbal tea

---

1 Vocabulary in Context

Talking about table items

These are the names of dishes, silverware, and other table items.
Use **bowl, cup,** and **glass** to talk about quantities of food.

1. bowl	**5.** knife	**9.** saucer
2. cup	**6.** napkin	**10.** soup spoon (tablespoon)
3. fork	**7.** plate	**11.** spoon (teaspoon)
4. glass	**8.** salt and pepper shakers	

2 Practice

Work with a partner. Ask a waiter or waitress for something. Use *a* or *some*.

A: Excuse me. May I have	a fork, / some bread, / please?
B: Sure. / Just a minute.	

1. spoon
2. glass of water
3. cup of coffee
4. sugar
5. knife
6. salad
7. bowl of soup
8. clean plate
9. slice of toast
10. napkin
11. salt
12. soup spoon

3 Presentation

Making comparisons with *even*

To form the comparative of short adjectives, follow these rules:

Spelling Rules for Adding -er	
1. For most adjectives, add **-er**.	cold → colder small → smaller
2. For words ending in **-e**, add **-r**.	nice → nicer white → whiter
3. For words ending in vowel + consonant, double the consonant and add **-er**.	big → bigger hot → hotter
4. For words ending in **-y**, change the **y** to **i** and add **-er**.	pretty → prettier healthy → healthier

A

Cristina's pretty, but on her wedding day she'll be **even prettier**.

B

Gino's healthy, but after his diet he'll be even **healthier**.

4 Practice

Write sentences using *even* + the comparative adjective. Complete *10* and *11* with your own ideas.

Mr. Brown / angry // Mrs. Brown

Mr. Brown is angry, but Mrs. Brown is even angrier.

1. Gino / heavy // his brother

2. This program / funny // "Three for Dinner"

3. Atlanta / sunny // Miami

4. Sam / friendly // Bob

5. My car / dirty // your car

6. New York / windy // Chicago

7. The math homework / easy // the science homework

8. Ted / healthy // Joyce

9. Today / cloudy // yesterday

10. I / ——— // my friend ———

11. ——— / ——— // ———

5 Presentation

Contrast of *some* and *any*

1. Can Gino have **any** ham on his diet?
   No, he can't have **any** ham, but he can have **some** chicken.

2. Did Gino have **any** butter?
   No, he didn't have **any** butter, but he had **some** toast.

3. Can Gino have **any** cream in his diet?
   No, he can't have **any** cream, but he can have **some** milk.

> EXCEPTION: When we offer food or help, we often use **some**:
>
> Would you like **some** coffee?

6 Practice

Work with a partner. You're trying to order food in a restaurant. Practice talking to the waiter. Ask and answer questions using *some* and *any*.

> baked potatoes // french fries
> CUSTOMER: Do you have any baked potatoes?
> WAITER: I'm sorry. We don't have any baked potatoes. Would you like some french fries?
> CUSTOMER: Yes, that will be fine.

1. fish // chicken
2. Swiss cheese // American cheese
3. oranges // grapes
4. oatmeal // dry cereal
5. cake // pie

6. rye bread // white bread
7. tea // coffee
8. peas // carrots
9. bacon // sausage
10. apple juice // tomato juice

7 Reentry

Expressions of frequency; questions with *how often*

Work with a partner. Take turns asking and answering questions.

> Gino ate cake when he was on his diet. // once a month
>
> A: How often did Gino eat cake when he was on his diet?
> B: Once a month.

1. Mr. Young reads the newspaper. // every night
2. Joan reads the help-wanted ads. // every day
3. The Navas go on trips. // every summer
4. Cristina played volleyball last year. // once a month
5. Gino played tennis when he was on his diet. // three times a week
6. He plays tennis now. // once a week
7. Susan studied when she was in high school. // two or three nights a week
8. She studies now that she's in college. // every night
9. Gino and Cristina go out together. // every Wednesday and Sunday
10. Sam goes to classes at night. // four nights a week

8 Interaction

Talk with a partner about what you eat for breakfast, lunch, and dinner.

> A: What do you usually have for ___*breakfast*___ ?
> B: I ___*usually*___ have ___*toast and coffee*___ , and I
>   sometimes have ___*a bowl of cereal*___ . What about you?
> A: Oh, I usually have ___*yogurt and fruit*___ .

9 Listening

First Listening

Number your paper from 1-5. Listen to the description of each person, and write the letter of the statement that is *true*.

1. **a.** Lisa is healthy.
   b. Lisa isn't very healthy.
   c. Lisa is a good basketball player.
2. **a.** Tom likes to eat.
   b. Tom should relax.
   c. Tom should be on a diet.
3. **a.** Mrs. Rivera is thin.
   b. Mrs. Rivera is heavy.
   c. Mrs. Rivera is sick.
4. **a.** Liz doesn't have any problems with her teeth.
   b. Liz doesn't take care of her teeth.
   c. Liz brushes her teeth.
5. **a.** Gino is very sick.
   b. Gino eats too much.
   c. Gino is very tired.

Second Listening

Now number your paper from 1-6. Listen to each description a second time and answer the questions.

1. What sports does Lisa participate in?
2. What are two of Tom's problems?
3. What are Mrs. Rivera's favorite foods?
4. How often does Liz go to the dentist?
5. How many cavities did Liz have last winter?
6. Why does Gino eat so much?

10 Reentry

One/ones; comparatives; *too*

Cristina and Gino are shopping for some things for their new apartment. They want everything to be perfect, so they ask to see many things. Make sentences using comparative adjectives and *one* or *ones*.

> table / big // small
> This table is too big. We'd like a smaller one.
>
> cups / expensive // cheap
> These cups are too expensive. We'd like some cheaper ones.

1. soup bowls / small // big
2. bread knife / short // long
3. cups / ugly // pretty
4. knives and forks / expensive // cheap
5. soup spoons / small // big
6. plates / big // small
7. salad bowl / small // big
8. glass sculpture / big // small
9. salt shaker / small // big
10. napkins / expensive // cheap

Useful vocabulary:

cheap = not expensive

11 Presentation

Irregular past tense: *begin, lose, feel, sleep*

Gino Leone is really happy. He **began** a diet last week and he **lost** four pounds. His friend Luis isn't very happy. He tried to diet, too, but he didn't lose any weight. Gino told him to go see Dr. Young. Luis **felt** bad about his weight, so he made an appointment with Dr. Young for Monday morning. But on Monday he **slept** late and missed his appointment.

12 Practice

Complete the sentences with the past tense of *begin*, *lose*, *feel*, or *sleep*.

1. Cristina was late for work because she _____ late.
2. Luis _____ a diet two weeks ago.
3. Sekila _____ unhappy because her family was far away.
4. Liz _____ working at the telephone company when she was 20.
5. Cristina wasn't on a diet, but she _____ two pounds last week.
6. Bob was late to the party because he _____ his car keys.
7. Adela _____ a new computer course last week.
8. Gino _____ happy because he was losing weight.
9. Gloria _____ really nervous about the exam.
10. I _____ studying English (a year) ago.

13 Presentation 🔲

More comparisons

Contrast these:	
***Some* + noncountable noun**	**Quantity + noncountable noun**
1. I'd like **some milk**.	1. I'd like **a quart of milk**.
2. I'd like **some water**.	2. I'd like **a glass of water**.
3. Would you like **some coffee**?	3. No, but I'd like **a cup of tea**.
4. I'd like **some soup**.	4. I'd like **a bowl of soup**.
5. Would you like **some bread**?	5. Yes, I'd like **a slice**, please.
6. Would you like **some steak**?	6. Yes, I'd like **a piece**, please.

14 Practice

Gino is having dinner at Cristina's apartment. He's trying to stay on his diet. He can only eat and drink the foods and beverages listed on pages 93-94. Cristina offers him different things to eat and drink. He only accepts the things on his diet. Complete the sentences below.

> CRISTINA: Would you like *some* dessert?
> GINO: Thanks. I'll have a *cup of fruit salad* .

1. CRISTINA: Would you like ____ juice?
   GINO: Yes, I'd like a _____ .

2. CRISTINA: Would you like ____ ham or ____ chicken?
GINO: Thanks, I'd like a _____ .

3. CRISTINA: Would you like ____ french fries?
GINO: No, thanks. Could I have a _____ , instead?

4. CRISTINA: Would you like ____ bread and butter?
GINO: Thanks. I'll just have a _____ .

5. CRISTINA: Would you like ____ cake or pie?
GINO: They look delicious, but I'd rather have a _____ .

6. CRISTINA: Would you like ____ coffee or ____ tea?
GINO: I'd love a _____ .

15 Interaction

Imagine that a friend has come to your home. Offer him or her some food. Practice the conversation with a partner. After you finish the conversation, go back and write the words you used. (Don't write while you are talking.)

HOST: Would you like something to drink? We have
_____ and _____ .
GUEST: Yes. I'd like | some | _____ .
| a glass of |
HOST: How about _____ to eat?
GUEST: Yes, thank you. I'd like _____ if you have any.
HOST: Certainly.
GUEST: This is very good.
HOST: Thank you. Why don't you also try some _____ ?
GUEST: _____ .
HOST: Would you like some more _____ ?
GUEST: _____ .

16 Reading

Before You Read

1. Did you or a friend ever go on a diet?

2. Did you (or your friend) ask for professional help? Who did you ask?

3. Did you (or your friend) stay on the diet and lose weight? Why or why not?

First Reading

Work with a partner. Discuss the meanings of the words or phrases listed below and match them to the correct definitions. Use context clues in the reading for help.

1. essential	**a.**	to work or operate
2. abundant	**b.**	to check
3. vital	**c.**	very important
4. initially	**d.**	at first
5. counselor	**e.**	a stage or period of time
6. stabilize	**f.**	a person who gives advice
7. monitor	**g.**	having lots of something
8. maintenance	**h.**	the study of food and diet
9. function	**i.**	keeping something the same
10. permanent	**j.**	to cause something to stay the same
11. scale	**k.**	absolutely necessary
12. behavior	**l.**	not changing
13. modification	**m.**	how a person acts
14. nutrition	**n.**	an instrument that gives the weight of a person or thing
15. phase	**o.**	a change

DIET CENTER'S
COMPREHENSIVE FIVE-PHASE PROGRAM

Diet Center offers a complete, comprehensive weight-control program consisting of a four-phase diet: Conditioning, Reducing, Stabilization, and Maintenance. A fifth phase, Nutrition/Behavior Modification Classes (NBMC), is taught daily at the scale and in weekly classes. Each phase is essential to your ultimate goal — permanent weight control! On the first visit, you and your counselor will establish your personal, ideal weight goal.

1. **Conditioning.** The two-day Conditioning Diet prepares the body for the most effective weight loss possible. A previous diet of processed foods, high in refined sugars and starches, is replaced with wholesome, natural foods, abundant in vital nutrients, complex carbohydrates and naturally occurring sugars as well as fiber and bulk.

2. **Reducing.** During this phase, you will meet privately, six days a week, with a professional Diet Center Counselor. You will be given a list of foods allowed on the program along with an eating schedule. Initially, your counselor will measure and weigh you, then your progress will be charted daily. She will also provide positive reinforcement to help you reach your weight goal.

3. **Stabilization.** This phase of the Diet Center Program is just as important as the Reducing Phase. You will remain on Stabilization one week for every two weeks spent on the Reducing Phase (up to three weeks.) You will come in twice a week for counseling sessions, and your counselor will expand your diet to a wider variety of wholesome foods in greater amounts. Your weight will be monitored closely, and permanent changes in eating habits will be reinforced. This phase of the program stabilizes your body at your new weight, which prepares you for permanent weight control. Stabilization is offered at no additional cost.

4. **Maintenance.** After you complete the Diet Center Stabilization Phase, you will be allowed to come to Diet Center for private counseling and continued support once a week until you feel comfortable with your new weight (up to 52 weeks.) Set up an appointment for the day you plan to come, and bring the previous week's food diary with you. There is no additional charge for the Maintenance Phase.

5. **Nutrition/Behavior Modification Classes.** The NBMC Series is essential to your success in achieving permanent weight control. Diet Center believes when you become educated in nutrition, you are then able to make wise, nutritional choices. You, and you alone, are responsible for yourself. Weekly classes are scheduled where you will be taught the principles of sound nutrition, self-direction, behavior modification, and exercise. You will learn how your body functions, how stress affects the body and how to deal with that stress. You will also learn meal planning and food preparation techniques that will help you as well as your family. Positive changes in eating habits will be reinforced to ensure permanent weight control. The NBMC Series is offered at no additional charge.

DIET CENTER'S MAIN OBJECTIVE IS:
PERMANENT WEIGHT CONTROL THROUGH SOUND NUTRITION

Second Reading

Read the selection again and answer these questions. Then discuss your answers in small groups.

1. What kinds of food do you eat during the Conditioning Diet?
2. How often do you meet with your counselor during the Reducing Phase of the diet?
3. Do you have to pay for the Stabilization Phase of the diet?
4. During the Maintenance Phase, for how many months can you continue to see your counselor?
5. How often are the Nutrition/Behavior Modification Classes taught?
6. Name two things you will learn in the Nutrition/Behavior Modification Classes.
7. Would you go to the Diet Center? Why or why not?

17 Writing

A. When Gino joined the Winfield Health Club, he had to fill out an application for membership. Fill out the membership application for yourself.

B. Then work in groups of three or four and compare your answers to questions 1, 2, and 3 in the application.

MEMBERSHIP APPLICATION

WHC

WINFIELD HEALTH CLUB
5286 Prince Street
Winfield, New York 11500

- swimming pool
- tennis courts
- exercise room
- running track

- health food restaurant
- aerobics classes
- group trips–skiing, mountain climbing, and many more

Name _____ **Date of Birth** _____

Address _____ **Height** _____

Telephone _____ **Weight** _____

Sex   **Occupation** _____
(Circle one)   MALE   FEMALE

Do you have any health problems? (If yes, please explain.)

_____

Interests

_____

1. Things you like to do: _____

_____

2. Things you'd like to learn how to do at the club: _____

_____

3. Trips you'd like to take with the club: _____

_____

DATE _____   SIGNATURE _____

18 Final Activity

STUDENT A: You are a customer in a restaurant. You are on the same diet as Gino (see pages 93-94). Study the menu on page 105 and choose one entree, one vegetable (you don't like broccoli), and one salad. Get a side order and beverage if you want, but no dessert because of your diet. You can use phrases like these:

I'd like _____ .   Is/Are the _____ good?
Do you have any _____ ?   What kind of _____ do you have?

STUDENT B: You are a waiter or waitress at The Corner Restaurant. You can only serve what is on the menu. Also, you are out of steak, broiled fish, green beans, and squash. Don't forget to offer your customer some dessert. (The waiter or waitress who sells the most desserts this week gets a $50.00 bonus!)

THE CORNER RESTAURANT
293 Cliff Road
Winfield, New York 11500
516-625-4980

Entrees

Turkey with baked potato $5.75
Baked chicken 6.50
Spaghetti and meatballs 5.25
Steak 8.95
Broiled fish 8.95
Hamburger 4.95

Vegetables

Asparagus $1.45
Broccoli .... .85
Green beans .... .90
Squash .... .95

Salads and Side Orders

Fruit salad $3.25
Tossed salad 2.50
Lettuce and tomato salad 1.50
French fries 1.85
Rice and beans 1.65
Chicken soup 1.25
Fruit (apple/pear/grapes) 1.35

Beverages

Soda $1.20
Tomato juice .... .75
Grapefruit juice .... .75
Milk 1.00
Coffee .... .90
Tea .... .90
Herbal tea 1.00

Desserts

Apple pie .... $ 1.75
Chocolate cake 1.50
Ice cream 1.25

Breakfast

Two eggs $1.65
Bacon 1.50
Cereal .... .95
Yogurt 1.15
Toast .... .80
Half grapefruit .... .95

COMMUNICATION	GRAMMAR
Talking about illness ▪ Talking about ability or possibility in the past ▪ Giving reasons ▪ Making comparisons	*Have/has, got* ▪ *Could* to express ability or possibility ▪ Irregular past tense: *cost, drink, forget, tell* ▪ Present perfect tense of *be* + adjective ▪ *Make* and *keep*
	SKILLS
	Describing symptoms to a doctor ▪ Reading health news ▪ Writing about a visit to the doctor

Another Visit to the Doctor

Cristina is at Dr. Young's office again.

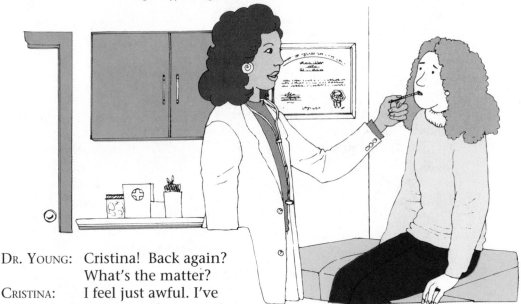

DR. YOUNG: Cristina! Back again? What's the matter?

CRISTINA: I feel just awful. I've got a sore throat and a headache. Everything hurts.

DR. YOUNG: Well, I'll take your temperature and see if you've got a fever. . . Hm, 102. Do you have a cough?

CRISTINA: No.

DR. YOUNG: An earache?

CRISTINA: No.

DR. YOUNG: A stomachache?

CRISTINA: No, just a sore throat and a headache, and I've been really depressed.

DR. YOUNG: How long have you been sick and depressed?

CRISTINA: I've been sick for about a week, and I've been really depressed for two or three days.

DR. YOUNG: You've probably got the flu, and that's making you depressed. There's a flu going around Winfield right now. I'll just examine your throat and listen to your chest. . . . Well, your throat's a little red, but your chest sounds OK. You should stay in bed and drink a lot of liquids. I'm going to prescribe some medicine for you. Take one pill four times a day for ten days. OK?

CRISTINA: OK. Thanks, Dr. Young. Bye.

DR. YOUNG: Not at all. Take it easy, Cristina — and cheer up! You don't want to be sick for your wedding . . . Oh, wait a minute! Don't forget the prescription for your medicine! You should ask the pharmacist to fill your prescription right away, so that you'll feel better as soon as possible.

1 Vocabulary in Context

Talking about illness

Cristina was **depressed** because she wasn't feeling well. Dr. Young took Cristina's **temperature**. It was high — the thermometer read 102°F. Then she **examined** Cristina's throat and saw that it was red inside. After the **examination,** Dr. Young said to Cristina, "I'm going to **prescribe** some **pills** for you." Dr. Young wrote down the **prescription** and gave it to Cristina. "You should **take the medicine** four times a day for ten days," said Dr. Young. "And don't forget to drink plenty of **liquids,** like juice or tea." Cristina went to the drugstore and the **pharmacist** took her prescription and gave her the medicine she needed.

2 Practice

Complete the paragraph with the correct words and expressions from *1*. Change the form of the word if necessary, and use each item only once.

Gloria was (1) _____ because she had an earache and it was the day before Cristina's wedding. She went to see Dr.Young, who (2) _____ her ears and took her (3) _____ . After the (4) _____ , Dr. Young (5) _____ some (6) _____ for her. Gloria took the (7) _____ to the drugstore. The (8) _____ said she had to (9) _____ three times a day with any (10) _____ except milk.

3 Presentation

Have got/Has got

> Use **have got** and **has got** just like **have** and **has**.

Contractions:

he's got = he has got
we've got = we have got

1. I have a problem. = I**'ve got** a problem.
2. You have the flu. = You**'ve got** the flu.
3. Gino has a great recipe. = He**'s got** a great recipe.
4. We have a good teacher. = We**'ve got** a good teacher.
5. They have a nice apartment. = They**'ve got** a nice apartment.

4 Practice

Look at the pictures. Then practice a conversation like the model. Practice the conversation several times, choosing a different problem each time.

> A: How are you doing?
> B: Not too well.
> A: What's the matter?
> B: I've got a bad headache.
> A: That's too bad. Maybe you should take some aspirin.
> B: Yeah, I think I will.
> A: I hope you feel better.
> B: Thanks.

1.
a stomachache

2.
a headache

3.
an earache

4.
a sore throat

5.
a cold

6.
a cough

7.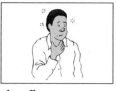

the flu

8.

a fever

9.

a backache

5 Presentation

Talking about ability or possibility with *could*

> To talk about ability or possibility in the past, use **could**.
> **Could** is the past of **can.**
>
> couldn't = could not
>
> **1.** There was a tennis game yesterday. Elinor **could** play, but Adela **couldn't** because she was sick.
> **2.** My throat was very sore yesterday. I **couldn't** talk, but I **could** eat.

6 Practice

Make a sentence using *can/can't* or *could/couldn't*.

> The water was very cold yesterday. // swim / play tennis
> We couldn't swim, but we could play tennis.

> It's very hot today. // play tennis / swim
> We can't play tennis, but we can swim.

  1. It was very cold yesterday. // swim / skate
  2. My brother is very nervous tonight. // study / listen to the radio
  3. My sister was sick last night. // eat / drink tea
  4. I'm too heavy. // eat cake / eat salads
  5. Lisa and Bob were sick. // go out / watch TV
  6. Sam is sick today. // work / read in bed
  7. Gino is on a diet this week. // eat butter / eat bread
  8. Nhu Trinh had a sore throat last night. // sing / talk softly
  9. Gloria has a headache tonight. // listen to the radio / eat
10. Cristina had a fever last week. // drink milk / drink tea

7 Practice

Work with a partner. Take turns asking and answering questions using *couldn't*
and *because*.

> play tennis today // too hot
> A: Did you play tennis today?
> B: No. I couldn't because it was too hot.

1. go to the supermarket yesterday // didn't have any money
2. go to the mountains last week // sick
3. play tennis this morning // raining
4. go on a vacation last month // too busy
5. go to Mike's party two weeks ago // on vacation
6. go skating yesterday // wasn't any ice
7. study last night // had to clean the house
8. do the dishes this morning // had to go to work early
9. go to the movies last night // sick
10. drive to New York last weekend // weather so bad

8 Interaction

Work with a partner. Take turns asking about what the other person did yesterday,
last night, last week, etc. Here's a model.

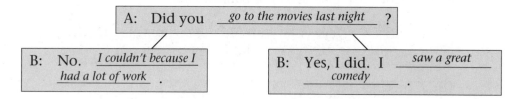

A: Did you _go to the movies last night_ ?

B: No. _I couldn't because I had a lot of work_ .

B: Yes, I did. I _saw a great comedy_ .

9 Presentation

Irregular past tense: *cost, drink, forget, tell*

Dr. Young comes into her office.
Read the conversation she has
with her receptionist, Jean.

DR. YOUNG: How are you doing, Jean?
JEAN: I'm really busy. We had a lot of phone calls this morning.
DR. YOUNG: Oh, who called?
JEAN: Let's see . . . Mrs. Alves. Her son hurt his leg, so she's
             bringing him in this afternoon. Mr. Alberti called, too. He
             felt terrible last night and slept badly. He said he **forgot**
             to take his pills. He'll call back. And then little Brenda
             Johnson **drank** some detergent, so I **told** her mother to
             take her to the hospital.
DR. YOUNG: Poor Brenda! Anybody else?
JEAN: Yes. Mrs. Khan called, too. She couldn't get her
             prescription because it **cost** too much. She wants you to
             call her.
DR. YOUNG: My goodness! You really have been busy.

10 Practice

Complete the conversation with the past tense of *buy, catch, cost, drink, feel,
forget, hurt, see, sleep, take,* or *tell.* You can use some of them more than once.

HOWARD: How was your day?
ELINOR: Pretty good, but busy. I (1) _____ a lot of patients. Bill
          Armstrong (2) _____ his arm skiing, and Marty Field's
          daughter (3) _____ a whole bottle of cough medicine, but
          she's OK now.
HOWARD: Did you see Cristina? She called here and I (4) _____ her to
          call the office.
ELINOR: Yeah. She's got the flu. She (5) _____ really depressed,
          but she looked better after I (6) _____ her.
HOWARD: And how's that guy — what's his name? Jasper?
ELINOR: Oh, Jasper Clinton. He's much better. He (7) _____ well
          last night. How was your day?
HOWARD: I was really tired, so I (8) _____ the bus home early. By the
          way, I (9) _____ to get something for Joyce's birthday.
ELINOR: Don't worry. I (10) _____ something for her — a sweater. It
          only (11) _____ $25.00. Do you like it?
HOWARD: It's beautiful!

11

Presentation 🔲

Present perfect tense of *be* + adjective

To describe a condition or situation that started in the past and is still continuing, use:
  present perfect of **be** + *adjective*

1. Cristina **has been** sick lately.
2. Gino and Cristina **have been** busy lately.

Contractions

I have been = I've been
you have been = you've been
he has been = he's been
she has been = she's been
it has been = it's been
we have been = we've been
they have been = they've been

12

Practice

Work with a partner. Ask and answer questions with a sentence using the present perfect of *be*.

Why does Cristina look so tired lately? // sick
A: Why does Cristina look so tired lately?
B: She's been sick.

1. Why does Gino look different? // on a diet

2. Why is Lee absent again? // sick

3. Why does Liz look so tired lately? // busy

4. Why is Betty so quiet today? // worried about her mother

5. I haven't seen you lately. How have you been? // very well

6. How are the children doing? // quiet all morning

7. Is your vacation going well? // wonderful

8. Doesn't Paul like you any more? // angry with me

9. How's the weather there lately? // cloudy

10. Why didn't Susan finish this? // sick all week

13 Listening

First Listening

Number your paper from 1-10. You will hear one speaker in a telephone conversation. Listen and write, *T* (True), *F* (False) or *NG* (Not Given) for each of the following sentences.

1. Tim is sick.
2. Tim is in Dr. Young's office.
3. Tim's father is sick.
4. Tim has an appointment for tomorrow morning.
5. Tim must stay in bed.
6. Tim should drink a lot of liquids.
7. Tim can watch TV.
8. Tim cannot take aspirin.
9. Tim can have chicken for dinner.
10. Tim shouldn't eat toast.

Second Listening

Now number your paper from 1-17. Work with two or three other students. Listen to Dr. Young again. Then write the conversation that the other person has with Dr. Young by completing the following sentences.

1. Dr. Young, this is _____ .
2. I'm calling about my _____ .
3. Yes, he's _____ .
4. Yes, he's got a _____ and a _____ .
5. No, he _____ .
6. Yes, he's got a bad _____ .
7. I'm sorry. I can't because _____ .
8. That's _____ .
9. _____ .
10. But Dr. _____ . . .
11. What should _____ ?
12. Can he _____ ?
13. All _____ ?
14. Yes, _____ .
15. What should he _____ ?
16. Should I give him some _____ ?
17. OK, Dr. Young. _____ very much.

Presentation 🔲

Make and **keep**

> Use **make** with a *simple* adjective (like *good, big, easy*) or with
> a *comparative* adjective (like *better, bigger, easier*) to talk about
> something that changes.
>
> Use **keep** with a *simple* adjective to show that something stays
> the same.

1. Having the flu can **make** you **depressed.**
2. Tom has the flu, but this medicine can **make** him **better.**
3. Gino lost a lot of weight. Exercise and good food will **keep** him **thin.**

15 **Practice**

Complete the sentences with the adjectives in the box. Some sentences have
more than one possible answer.

angry	happy	hungry	sad
busy	healthy	sick	unhappy
fat	heavy	thin	warm

1. Rainy days make me _____ .

2. A lot of exercise can make you _____ .

3. If you eat a lot of french fries, they can make you _____ .

4. A fire keeps you _____ .

5. Good friends can make you _____ .

6. Children can keep you very _____ .

7. Some movies make people _____ .

8. Salads and vegetables can keep you _____ .

9. A diet can make you _____ .

10. A lot of work can make a busy person _____ .

16 Reentry

Making comparisons

Complete the sentences with the comparative form of the adjective or adverb.

> Gino is (happy) ____happier____ now than he was two months ago.
> Gino is happier now than he was two months ago.

1. Gino lost twelve pounds, so he's in (good) _____ shape than he was before his diet.

2. Before his diet, Gino was (heavy) _____ than he is now.

3. Gino started by eating (small) _____ meals and (few) _____ snacks.

4. Now he can work (hard) _____ and run (fast) _____ than he could before.

5. He needs new clothes because he's (thin) _____ .

6. Cristina's nervous right now, but she'll be (calm) _____ after the wedding.

7. Cristina's got the flu, but she'll feel (good) _____ after she takes her medicine.

8. If people want to look (young) _____ and feel (healthy), _____ they should eat good food and exercise every day.

9. Nobody wants to be in (bad) _____ shape than when they were (young) _____ .

10. If you take care of your health, you'll feel (happy) _____ .

17 Reading

Before You Read

1. What should people do to help prevent heart problems?
2. Do you know what the difference is between whole milk and skim milk?
3. How can you keep your bathroom free from germs?

Useful vocabulary:

1. **antibiotic:** a kind of medicine. Penicillin is an antibiotic.

2. **bacteria:** microscopic organisms. Some bacteria cause disease.

3. **cholesterol:** a substance found in animal fats. Too much cholesterol is bad for your heart.

4. **quart:** a liquid measure. A quart is about the same amount as a liter.

5. **reduce:** to make less. If you reduce calories, you will lose weight.

6. **skim milk:** milk without fat. When you remove the fat from whole milk, the result is skim milk.

First Reading

Skim the three short articles about health and fitness. (When you skim, you read very quickly to get the *main* idea of a text.) Then choose the correct main idea for each article.

1. In the article "Help Your Heart," the most important way to prevent heart problems is to:

   a. stop smoking.

   b. exercise regularly.

   c. lower your cholesterol.

2. In the article "If You Like Milk - Choose the Right Milk!", the most important reason to drink skim milk is:

   a. it can lower your cholesterol.

   b. it makes your blood pressure go down.

   c. you will not get fat.

3. The article "Watch That Toothbrush!" gives advice about when to:

   a. clean your bathroom.

   b. take an antibiotic.

   c. change toothbrushes.

Help Your Heart

We all know that it's a good idea to stop smoking, reduce our cholesterol, control our high blood pressure, and get regular exercise. These are important ways to prevent heart problems. We all know this, but . . .

The Centers for Disease Control in Atlanta, Georgia, say that 60 percent of Americans are in danger of heart disease because they don't get enough physical exercise.

What can you do? That's easy — start a physical exercise program. You should exercise at least three times a week and for at least 20 minutes each time. Do it! Your heart will thank you!

If You Like Milk - Choose the Right Milk!

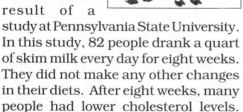

Skim milk can lower your cholesterol. This is the result of a study at Pennsylvania State University. In this study, 82 people drank a quart of skim milk every day for eight weeks. They did not make any other changes in their diets. After eight weeks, many people had lower cholesterol levels. Why? The study leaders think that the lower cholesterol is because of the composition of skim milk. Thirty-nine of the people in the study started with high cholesterol levels; these same people had less cholesterol at the end of the study. Many of the people in the study also had a lower blood pressure at the end of the study.

And guess what! No one in the study gained weight!

Watch That Toothbrush!

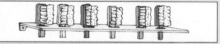

Do you think that your bathroom is a very clean place? You may be wrong. A recent study at the University of Oklahoma discovered a lot of problems in bathrooms. This study looked at people with pneumonia, strep throat, diarrhea, sinus diseases, and ulcers. Some people in the study changed their toothbrush every two weeks. They also took the antibiotics their doctors prescribed. Other people in the study took the right medicines, but they did not change their toothbrushes. People who changed their toothbrushes got better much faster than people who did not change their toothbrushes. What does this mean? Researchers think that the bacteria on old toothbrushes made people sicker.

So what should you do? If you are sick, you should throw away your old toothbrush and buy a new one!

Reread the three articles carefully and answer these questions.

1. What four things should you do to prevent heart disease?
2. Which of these four things do many Americans *not* do?
3. How often should you exercise, and for how long each time?
4. What did the people in the Pennsylvania State University cholesterol study do?
5. What happened to the people who started the study with high cholesterol levels?
6. What other benefits did the people in the study get from drinking skim milk?
7. In the University of Oklahoma study, what two things helped people feel better faster?
8. When should you throw away your toothbrush?

18 Writing

Write about your last visit to a doctor — a real visit or an imaginary one.

1. Plan what to write. Think about these questions, and make notes:
   • Why did you see the doctor?
   • What kinds of questions did he or she ask?
   • What instructions and/or information did the doctor give you? Did you follow them?
2. Write three paragraphs about your experience. In the first paragraph explain why you went to the doctor. In the second paragraph describe what happened at the doctor's office. In the third paragraph, say whether you followed the doctor's advice or not.

19 Final Activity

Work with a partner and take turns talking about a recent illness. Ask about:
   • **your partner's symptoms**
   • **what he/she did about them**
   • **what things he/she could or couldn't do**
If your partner hasn't been sick, talk about what he/she does to stay healthy. Then describe the results to the class.

> Peter was sick last month. He had a fever and a cough. He took aspirin and stayed in bed. He couldn't go to work for a week.

COMMUNICATION
Describing a wedding ▪ Talking about what makes you nervous ▪ Talking about gifts ▪ Shopping for household items

SKILLS
Writing a thank-you note ▪ Reading a wedding announcement

GRAMMAR
Preposition: *for* + indirect object: statements and questions ▪ Separable phrasal verbs ▪ *Get* + adjective ▪ *Get* + noun

Cristina and Gino Get Married

At the wedding in St. Mark's Church:

It was a beautiful, cool fall day. The colorful leaves made a spectacular background for the wedding party. Gino, the proud groom, was dressed in an elegant tuxedo. He stood silently as he waited anxiously for his bride to enter the church. The best man, Gino's friend, Luis, who works with him at the Roma, was also waiting at the altar.

*Mr. and Mrs Eduardo Silva
invite you to be present
at the marriage of their daughter*

*Cristina Ana
to
Mr. Gino Antonio Leone*

*on Saturday, the fifth of October
nineteen hundred and ninety-one
at four o'clock
Saint Mark's Chapel
Winfield, New York*

*Reception to follow
at the Roma Restaurant*

R.S.V.P.

Cristina's mother walked into the church first. Then, the two bridesmaids entered the church, followed by the maid of honor, Cristina's sister Carmen. Excitement was in the air, as the wedding procession continued.

And finally, the moment the guests had all been waiting for — Cristina's father walked in with his daughter at his side. Cristina walked slowly down the aisle while the wedding march played. Cristina was a beautiful bride. She wore a long white gown with a long veil of lace.

Gino and Cristina's friends were happy to be at the wedding. Many of them whispered comments to each other.

"Doesn't Cristina look gorgeous! Oh, women always look so beautiful on their wedding day!"

"Isn't Gino a handsome young man! I just love weddings! They're so romantic!"

"What a beautiful wedding! What a good-looking couple! I'm so glad I was invited."

"Me, too. I've been looking forward to this day for a long time!"

1 Vocabulary in Context

Describing a wedding

Complete the sentences below with the correct word or expression from the list.

best man	maid of honor
bride	reception
bridesmaid	tuxedo
couple	veil
gown	wedding party
groom	

1. A type of suit that men wear to weddings and formal parties is called a _____ .

2. The woman getting married is called the _____ .

3. The bride and groom, the maid of honor, the best man, and the bridesmaids are called the _____ .

4. The _____ at Gino's wedding was his friend Luis.

5. The _____ at the wedding was Cristina's sister Carmen.

6. A _____ is also a female member of the wedding party.

7. Cristina wore a beautiful white _____ .

8. A bride usually wears a _____ on her head.

9. The party after the wedding is called the _____ .

10. The man getting married is called the _____ .

11. Two people married to each other are called a _____ .

2 Reentry

Asking for information

Work with a partner. Look at the invitation to Gino and Cristina's wedding, on page 119. Ask and answer questions using *who*, *where*, and *when*.

> NOTE: R.S.V.P. (*French*: <u>R</u>épondez <u>S</u>'il <u>V</u>ous <u>P</u>laît) means that the person who receives the invitation should give an answer.

3 Presentation

For + indirect object

> Some common verbs that need **for** before an indirect object are: **buy, cook, find, get, make, prepare.**

1. Gino **found** a beautiful wedding ring **for Cristina.**
2. The guests **bought** wedding gifts **for Cristina and Gino.**
3. The Roma Restaurant **prepared** dinner **for 100 guests.**

4 Practice

Make past tense statements with *for*.

> Cristina / buy a beautiful necklace / her mother-in-law
> Cristina bought a beautiful necklace for her mother-in-law.

1. Gino / cook / a special meal / his friends
2. Carmen / find / a small sculpture by Chang Ling / Cristina and Gino
3. Cristina and Carmen / prepare / the flowers / the bridesmaids
4. Cristina / make / a list of the wedding guests / her parents
5. Gino and Cristina / prepare / wedding invitations / 100 guests
6. Mrs. Silva / make / a Colombian wedding cake / Cristina and Gino
7. Mr. Silva / buy / a pair of beautiful gold earrings / his daughter
8. Gino's parents / get / an elegant Italian suit / their son
9. The bridesmaids / buy / beautiful glasses / Cristina and Gino
10. Gino / get / a silver ring / his best man

Presentation

Questions with *for* + indirect object

A

A:	Who did Cristina buy a necklace **for?**
B:	**For** her new mother-in-law.

B

A:	What did Cristina buy **for** her mother-in-law?
B:	A beautiful necklace.

6 **Practice**

Work with a partner. Ask and answer questions with *for* using the information in *4*. Use the models in *5*.

7 **Presentation**

Separable phrasal verbs

> Phrasal verbs are two- or three-word verb phrases with a special meaning. Some of these verbs can be separated. There are two possible positions for the objects of separable phrasal verbs.

A

Gino and Cristina **picked out** the wedding invitations. OR
Gino and Cristina **picked** the wedding invitations **out.**

B

Before the wedding, Luis **picked up** the flowers. OR
Before the wedding, Luis **picked** the flowers **up.**

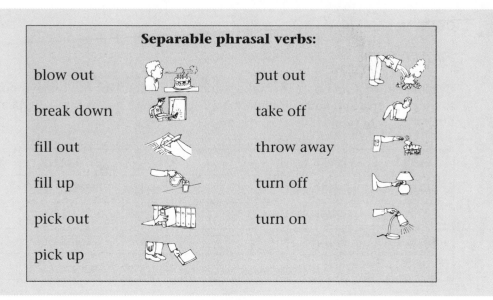

Separable phrasal verbs:

blow out		put out	
break down		take off	
fill out		throw away	
fill up		turn off	
pick out		turn on	
pick up			

8 Practice

Complete the sentences with the correct tense and form of a separable phrasal verb.

> The car was cold, so Elinor ___*turned on*___ the heat.

1. Lisa will _____ the candles on her birthday cake.
2. The firefighters had to _____ the door to rescue the child.
3. Bob _____ the TV because he wanted to study.
4. Cristina _____ a form for her driver's license.
5. Carmen _____ a beautiful present for Cristina and Gino.
6. Gloria went to the drugstore to _____ her prescription.
7. Cristina _____ her ring to show it to her mother.
8. Last week Luis had to _____ a fire in the Roma's kitchen.
9. When the Logans get gasoline, they always _____ their car.
10. Don't _____ the newspaper. I want to read it!

9 Practice

Separate the phrasal verbs in *8* and make new sentences.

> The car was cold, so Elinor turned on the heat.
>
> The car was cold, so Elinor turned the heat on.

Listening ⊙▭⊙

First Listening

Cristina called Tom Logan to make plane reservations for her honeymoon. Listen to the conversation and complete the air travel chart below for Cristina and Gino's itinerary.

DATE	LEAVE	TIME	ARRIVE	TIME	AIRLINE
Oct. 6	New York	6:25 PM	Paris	7:45 AM	TWA
	Paris				Alitalia
Oct. 19	Naples		Rome	10:00 AM	
			New York		TWA

Second Listening

Now, number your paper from 1–20. Listen to the conversation again and fill in the missing words.

TOM: Good morning. Wells Travel Agency.

CRISTINA: Hello, Tom. This (1) _____ Cristina Silva.

TOM: Hi, Cristina. All ready (2) _____ the wedding?

CRISTINA: Well, almost. In fact, I'm calling (3) _____ make plane reservations for our honeymoon.

TOM: Great. Where (4) _____ you going?

CRISTINA: To Paris, Rome, and Naples. We need reservations (5) _____ the trip there and back.

TOM: Are you planning to leave (6) _____ New York City?

CRISTINA: Yes. We'd like (7) _____ leave on . . . uhmm . . . October 6th and return (8) _____ October 19th.

TOM: Let's see. There's a flight on TWA. It leaves . . . just a minute . . . (9) _____ 6:25 PM from Kennedy Airport and arrives at Paris at (10) _____ the next morning. How long do you want to stay (11) _____ Paris?

CRISTINA: Three days.

TOM: OK. Then you can take an Alitalia flight from Paris to Rome on October (12) _____ . There's a good flight at (13) _____ PM. It arrives in (14) _____ at 2:10 in the afternoon. How long will you be in Rome?

CRISTINA: Well, we'd like to be there for three days so we can see the sights.

TOM:	Good idea. Then you'll leave Rome on October (15) _____ . Do you want to fly to Naples?
CRISTINA:	No, we'd like to take the train. Gino will get the tickets in Rome.
TOM:	Fine. Now for your return flight. There's an Alitalia flight from Naples to Rome at (16) _____ AM on October 19th, arriving at 10:00. You change to the TWA flight departing from Rome at (17) _____ PM. and arriving at New York, Kennedy, at 2:55 PM. How does that sound?
CRISTINA:	Wonderful! Is (18) _____ OK if I stop by the office in a few days to pick up the tickets?
TOM:	Sure. The fare (19) _____ two round-trip tickets comes to $2,200. Oh, and I guess I should write (20) _____ name as Cristina Leone on the ticket?
CRISTINA:	Oh, yes. I'll be Mrs. Leone by then.

11 Presentation

Get + adjective

> **Get** means *become* when used before an adjective.

1. When Cristina takes a train, she **gets nervous.**
2. I felt fine on Monday, but I **got sick** on Tuesday.
3. It's almost summer. The weather is **getting hot.**

12 Practice

Complete the sentences with the correct tense and form of *get* and one of the following adjectives:

angry	hungry	nervous	tired	wet
cool	late	ready	sick	worried

1. Gino and Cristina worked very hard on their wedding. They _____ .
2. Gino and Cristina went shopping on a rainy day, so they _____ .
3. Gino didn't eat breakfast or lunch, so he _____ before dinner time.
4. Gino _____ because Cristina didn't eat.

5. "Please take care of yourself," said Gino to Cristina. "I don't want you to _____ for our wedding!"
6. By October, the time of the wedding, the weather in Winfield _____ .
7. When Carmen arrived at Cristina's apartment, Cristina was _____ for the wedding.
8. Cristina's mother _____ , because Carmen was late.
9. "We should hurry up because it's _____ ," said Mrs. Silva.
10. Cristina was _____ because she didn't want to be late for her wedding.

13 Interaction

Talk with another student about what makes you nervous.

A: I get nervous when _____ .
B: Oh, really? Well, I get nervous when _____ .

14 Presentation

Get + noun

> **Get** can mean *receive, obtain, start to have,* or *buy* before a noun.

1. Elinor **got a phone call** from her travel agent.
2. She had to **get a passport** for her trip.
3. I don't feel well. I'm **getting a headache.**
4. Sekila went to the store to **get a newspaper.**

15 Practice

Complete the sentences with the correct tense and form of *get* and a noun from the list.

Nouns	
airline tickets	a computer game
a sore throat	a wedding invitation
a good job	a pair of silk shoes
a newspaper	a beautiful ring
the flu	a lot of presents

When Sam finishes college, he wants to ___get a good job___ .

1. Lisa _____ for Christmas last year.

2. Tom wants to read the news, so he's going to the store to _____ .

3. After she graduates from the technical institute, Adela will try to _____ .

4. Ted was playing football without his jacket, so he _____ .

5. The Youngs _____ from Cristina and Gino.

6. Gloria is tired and depressed. Maybe she's _____ .

7. Gino and Cristina _____ for their new home.

8. Gino _____ for Cristina.

9. Cristina _____ to match her wedding gown.

10. Cristina and Gino _____ as a wedding present from Cristina's parents.

16 Interaction

Ask another student what he or she received as a gift on some special occasion—a birthday, his/her wedding, or a special holiday. Include a comment about the gift.

A: What did you get for ___your birthday___ ?
B: I got ___a watch___ .
A: What a ___wonderful___ gift. ___Now you'll never be late___ .

17 Vocabulary in Context

Shopping for household items

Cristina and Gino had to buy many things for their new home. They made a list of the **household items** they needed:

1. towels

2. sheets

3. tablecloth

4. blender

5. vase

6. toaster

7. crystal glasses

8. casserole dishes

9. serving dishes

18 Practice

Complete the paragraph with the words from *17*.

Gino and Cristina were shopping at Warner's Department Store. They were looking at (1) _____ .

"Oh, look at this beautiful lace (2) _____ !" said Cristina. "It's perfect for a dinner party, and the (3) _____ we bought yesterday would look beautiful on it. And look, what a pretty (4) _____ this is — flowers would look beautiful in it."

Gino said, "Let's think about it. Why don't we look at kitchen things now? We still need a (5) _____ for breakfast, and a (6) _____ to make sauces. And for cooking we need several (7) _____ . Maybe we also need more (8) _____ to serve food when we have dinner parties."

"Fine, " said Cristina. "Now can we look at the bed and bathroom shop? Don't forget, that we need to buy (9) _____ for the bed and (10) _____ for the bathroom."

Cristina and Gino bought a lot of things for their new home, but they still need more things!

19 Writing

Gino and Cristina received many nice wedding gifts. Cristina wrote thank-you notes for the gifts. Here is one thank-you note:

> Dear Linda,
>   Thank you so much for the beautiful casserole dish. It is just what we needed because we don't have any serving dishes. Last night we had a big spaghetti dinner that Gino cooked, and our friends all liked the casserole dish (and the food)! We will think of you every time we use the dish. We're so glad you were able to come to the wedding and share our special day.
>   Love,
>   Cristina and Gino

Some of the other gifts that Cristina and Gino received were:

green bath towels
green and white sheets
blue and white dishes
a lace tablecloth

an electric knife
a blender
a crystal vase
a toaster

Select one of these gifts and write a thank-you note for it.

20 Reentry

In and *for*

Complete the following paragraph with *in* or *for*.

Gloria wants to go on a diet, but she doesn't want to start now. She wants to start (1) _____ a week. She's going to stay on the diet (2) _____ four weeks. She plans to lose 10 pounds (3) _____ four weeks. Gloria will also have to exercise. She plans to run (4) _____ 30 minutes (5) _____ the evening after school. She'll also get up at 6:30 (6) _____ the morning so she can do some exercises (7) _____ 20 minutes before school. When the diet is over (8) _____ four weeks, Gloria's going to buy a new dress!

Reading

Before You Read

1. Do you read the wedding announcements in the newspaper?
2. Why do you think people put wedding announcements in the newspaper?
3. Would/Did you put a wedding announcement in the newspaper for your own wedding? Why or why not?

First Reading

Scan the information in the wedding announcement. Then work with two or three classmates. Discuss the following words and phrases, and decide on the probable meaning for each. Work together to write sentences with each word or phrase. Compare your sentences with those of another group.

1. off-white
2. bouquet
3. flower girl
4. ushers
5. currently
6. reside

Julie Elizabeth Johnson Weds William Patrick Harris, Jr.

On February 9, Julie Elizabeth Johnson, daughter of Mr. and Mrs. Charles Johnson of Los Angeles, California, became the bride of William Patrick Harris, Jr., son of Dr. William Patrick Harris, Sr. of Washington, D.C., and Mrs. Donald Young, of Pittsburgh, Pennsylvania. The wedding took place at the Church of the Little Flower in Bethesda, Maryland.

Escorted by her father, the bride wore her mother's gown of off-white satin and lace with delicate beading and embroidered roses at the neckline and down the front. She carried a bouquet of pink and white roses.

Cynthia Johnson of Portland, Oregon, was maid of honor for her sister. The bride's other sister, Mrs. Susana Roberts, and the groom's sisters, Rebecca Harris of Hartford, Connecticut, and Mrs. Mary Jane Fisher, who also sang at the ceremony, served as bridesmaids. The bride's niece, Catherine Roberts, was flower girl. All the bridal attendants wore dresses of pale pink silk, and carried bouquets of pink and white spring flowers.

Michael James Harris of San Francisco, California, served as best man for his brother. The ushers included David Johnson, brother of the bride, and Robert Smith, Alan Jones, and Andrew Gaines.

The new Mrs. Harris graduated from National Cathedral School and George Washington University. She is a jewelry designer.

Mr. Harris is a graduate of St. Albans School and Georgetown University, and holds an M.A. from the University of Pennsylvania. He was formerly a newspaper correspondent and is currently a novelist.

A dinner dance reception at the Kenwood Club followed the ceremony. After their honeymoon in Jamaica, Mr. and Mrs. Harris will reside in Arlington, Virginia.

Second Reading

Read the announcement again. Then work with two or three classmates to write answers to these questions.

1. Who are the parents of the bride?

2. Who are the parents of the groom? Explain.

3. Who was the best man?

4. Did the bride wear a new dress? Explain.

5. Which bridesmaid provided music at the wedding?

6. What color were the bridesmaids' dresses?

7. What did the guests do at the wedding reception?

8. How many sisters does Julie have?

9. Who is the mother of the flower girl?

10. Where will the bride and groom live?

22 | Final Activity

Prepare an oral report that describes a wedding in your native country. Be sure to include the following information:

- Who decides if a couple will get married? The couple? The parents? Other people?
- How do the families tell other people about the marriage?
- How do the bride and groom and their families get ready for the wedding?
- What happens at the wedding ceremony?
- Is there a party or reception after the ceremony? Describe it.
- Do people give presents to the bride and groom? If so, what are some typical presents?
- Do the bride and groom go on a honeymoon? If so, what would be a typical honeymoon place?
- What other important things happen?

Share your oral report with classmates. Discuss what is the same and what is different about weddings in different countries.

<table>
<tr><td>

COMMUNICATION
Planning a vacation • Giving additional information • Making comparisons • Identifying someone • Talking about occupations

</td><td>

GRAMMAR
Relative clauses with *that* • Comparative adjective + *than any other* • *As + a/an +* noun • Irregular past tense: *draw, fall (down), hide, hit, ring, sit (down), tear, write*

SKILLS
Reading travel information • Writing a postcard or letter about a trip

</td></tr>
</table>

Vacation Plans

Cristina and Gino had to decide where to go for their honeymoon. Here are some of the travel ads they looked at.

——— PARIS
The Romantic City

MACHU PICCHU

The Vacation of a Lifetime

Walk where the Incas walked! Come to Machu Picchu, the historic city that is high in the mountains of Peru. You'll enjoy the fascinating ruins of this ancient city as well as the spectacular views.

Sun and Fun in Rio

If you love the tropical sun, Rio de Janeiro is a city that you will adore . . . Rio has everything — sandy white beaches, exciting nightlife, luxury hotels, and excellent restaurants. For more information, call your travel agent or H & H Holidays, Inc. (1-800-305-6792).

Come to ———
Canada

Canada is the friendly country that is close to home. You'll arrive as a tourist, but you'll leave as a friend. Ski on our snowy mountaintops and swim in our clear blue lakes. Enjoy the clean air of the country and the excitement of our cities.

JAPAN
Tokyo and Osaka

8 days/7 nights
$1589 (air fare not included)

Land of modern cities and ancient temples. Spend three exciting days in Tokyo. Then travel to Osaka on the bullet train — the famous train that is faster than any other train in the world. You'll love Osaka's museums and theaters, its history, and its great food.

1 Vocabulary in Context

Planning a vacation

adore	luxury	sandy
ancient	nightlife	spectacular
clear	romantic	temple
excitement	ruins	tropical

Complete the sentences with the correct word, changing the form if necessary.

Jamaica!

Come to our beauiful island! Walk on our (1 _____ beaches, enjoy our (2) _____ weather, swim in our (3) _____ blue sea. As evening falls, watch our (4) _____ sunsets. Or — for real (5) _____— try dancing the limbo!

Eternal Rome

Everyone (6) _____ Rome! This (7) _____ city has something for everyone. Try the exciting (8) _____ in our (9) _____ clubs and hotels, or enjoy the beautiful and (10) _____ fountains of Rome. Or learn about history — visit the (11) _____ of the Colosseum and ancient Roman (12) _____ . Rome has everything!

2 Reentry

Talking about future plans

Cristina and Gino are thinking about what they're going to do on their honeymoon. Make sentences using *going to*.

Cristina and Gino are going to fly to Europe.

1.

2.

3.

4.

3 Presentation

Giving additional information

To give additional information about a noun, use: **that** + a descriptive clause.

1. Rio is a city **that you will adore.**
2. Machu Picchu is a **city that is high in the mountains of Peru.**
3. The bullet train is a train **that is faster than any other train in the world.**

Expand the following sentences by adding a descriptive clause with *that*. Write your new sentences on a separate piece of paper. Then sit in groups of three or four and compare your sentences.

> A cat is an animal.
>
> A cat is an animal that likes to play.

1. Rio de Janeiro is a city.
2. Canada is a country.
3. Basketball is a sport.
4. Coffee is a drink.
5. Breakfast is a meal.

6. The Amazon is a river.
7. Carrots are vegetables.
8. Crime is a problem.
9. Jamaica is a vacation spot.
10. " . . . " is a TV program.

5 **Interaction**

Interview a classmate to find out about a vacation he or she *would like to* take. Ask at least five of the questions below.

> A: Where would you like to go on your vacation?
> B: To Japan.
> A: Oh, really? Why?
> B: Because I want to ride on the bullet train.

Interview Questions:

1. Where would you like to go on your vacation? Why?
2. What time of year would you like to travel? Why?
3. Who would you like to travel with? Why?
4. How would you like to travel? Why?
5. What tourist places would you like to see? Why?
6. What kind of food would you like to eat? Why?
7. What would you like to buy? Why?
8. How long would you like to stay? Why?

6 Presentation

Making comparisons

> To show that something is "the most," use:
> a comparative adjective + **than any other.**

1. The bullet train is **faster than any other** train in the world.
2. Mount Everest is **higher than any other** mountain in the world.

7 Practice

Use the cues and your own ideas to make sentences. Use a comparative adjective + *than any other.*

> New York City / large / city in the United States
> New York City is larger than any other city in the United States.

1. George / smart / student in this school
2. The Amazon / long / river in South America
3. Mr. Universe / strong / man in the contest
4. December 21st / short / day of the year in the northern hemisphere
5. Yesterday / hot / day of the summer
6. "My Children" / funny / family show on TV
7. *Romeo and Juliet* / sad / love story in history
8. The Sears Tower / tall / building in the world

8 Presentation

Identifying someone

> To indicate a person's occupation or identity, use: **as** + **a/an** + noun.

1. Toshio works **as a flight attendant** for Japan Air Lines.
2. Cristina works in an Italian restaurant **as a cashier.**
3. In Canada you arrive **as a tourist,** but you leave **as a friend.**

9 Practice

Make a sentence about the person's occupation using *as* and a noun.

> Ellen worked in Chicago. She was a police officer.
>
> Ellen worked in Chicago as a police officer.
> Ellen worked as a police officer in Chicago.

1. Howard works for a small engineering company. He's an engineer.

2. Sam works in Winfield. He's a mechanic.

3. Liz is going to work for an international airline. She's going to be a ticket agent.

4. Tom works in Winfield. He's a travel agent.

5. Gino works at an Italian restaurant. He's a chef.

6. Carla worked in Brazil. She was an English teacher.

7. John works for the *Winfield News*. He's a reporter.

8. Paul works for the telephone company. He's an accountant.

9. Maria works for the New York City Ballet. She's a dancer.

10. Kim works for a bank. She's a teller.

10 Interaction

Work with a partner. Ask about the occupations of people you know until you have a list of at least five different occupations. Then, as a class, put the lists together to see how many different occupations there are.

A: What does _____ do?				
B: _____ works as	a an	_____	in at for	_____ .

11 Presentation

Irregular past tense: *draw, fall (down), hide, hit, ring, sit (down), tear, write*

The Wrights are on vacation in "sunny California" and it's raining. It rained all day yesterday and the day before, too. It's cold and damp, and the Wright kids are going crazy. First Alice **hit** Steve. Then she **tore** her dress. Steve **drew** a great big picture— on the wall of the hotel room. Then he **hid** Alice's toys. The telephone **rang** and Alice **fell down** when she ran to answer it. Mrs. Wright was really feeling depressed, but she **sat down** and **wrote** a postcard to her sister in New York. It said, "Having a wonderful time!" Mr. Wright smiled at his wife and said, "Tomorrow we'll have better weather."

12 Practice

Complete the paragraph with the past tense of *draw, fall, hide, hit, ring, sit, tear, write.*

Nancy Gomez is a second-grade teacher, and yesterday was her first day of school. She had a really hard day. When the bell (1) _____ , Nancy said, "OK, boys and girls, take your seats." But none of the kids (2) _____ down, and she had to yell at them. One girl (3) _____ a picture of Nancy on the chalkboard while another girl (4) _____ the box of chalk. Then a boy (5) _____ his friend and ran outside. His friend chased him, (6) _____ down, and (7) _____ a big hole in the knee of his pants. Another boy (8) _____ some bad words on his desk. Nancy isn't sure she's going to like this class.

Gloria went to Brazil on vacation. When she returned home, she told her friend Sekila about it. Listen to their conversation.

First Listening

Number your paper from 1-6. Look at the list of topics that Gloria talks about. Decide whether they were good things or bad things on the trip. After listening to their conversation, write *good* or *bad*.

1. her flight to Rio
2. the sunset over Rio
3. her photos of Rio
4. her bathing suit
5. Brazilian food
6. her weight

Second Listening

Number your paper from 1-6 and write the letter of the correct answer.

1. At what time did Gloria arrive in Rio?
   a. at 8 PM
   b. at 6 PM
   c. at 8 AM

2. What is Sugar Loaf?
   a. a statue
   b. a sunset
   c. a mountain

3. What happened to Gloria's camera?
   a. She forgot it.
   b. It wasn't working.
   c. Someone stole it.

4. Why didn't Gloria like one of the pictures?
   a. She looked fat.
   b. She didn't like her bathing suit.
   c. She wasn't smiling.

5. Why did Gloria like the restaurants in Rio?
  a. The food was good.
  b. The music was good.
  c. The people were friendly.

6. Which is *not* a reason that Gloria enjoyed her vacation?
  a. She met friendly people.
  b. She lost weight.
  c. She saw many interesting sights.

14 Writing

Write a postcard or a letter to a friend about a special place you visited. Tell about some of these things: when you went, who was with you, what you saw, why it was interesting, how you felt when you were there, why you would like to return there.

To:

_____

_____

_____

_____

15 Reading

Before You Read

1. Where is San Francisco?

2. Do you know what is special about San Francisco?

3. What important things should a city have?

First Reading

Look at the map of San Francisco. As you read, follow the route of the day's tour on the map. Then work with a partner and describe what you did at each place. Listen to your partner's description. Did you do the same things?

A Day's Tour of San Francisco

Where to stay in San Francisco? The possibilities are endless, but if you stay at a hotel near Union Square, you'll have lots of things to see just a short distance away. There are small hotels here in the heart of San Francisco within walking distance of the Financial District, Union Square stores, world-famous restaurants, theaters, Chinatown, and many of the other places people like to visit in the "City by the Bay." Some are expensive, some are fairly reasonable, and all are close to a cable car stop.

Begin your tour at the corner of Powell and Market Streets with a ride on one of the famous cable cars that are used for transportation by both tourists and residents. Take the car down to the Fisherman's Wharf area, where there's a festive atmosphere year-round. You'll find great street entertainment, colorful shops, and interesting old buildings. Then walk down Columbus Avenue to North Beach and have lunch at one of the many delightful Italian cafés. If you like

a good climb, walk over to Telegraph Hill, where you can get a spectacular view of the city and the bay.

Just south of North Beach is Chinatown. For a fascinating look at the

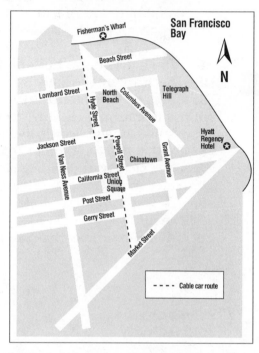

largest Chinese neighborhood outside Asia, walk down Grant Avenue. After visiting Chinatown, turn left on California Street and walk to the end of the street, where you'll see the Hyatt Regency, a modern luxury hotel. If you're there on a Friday evening, you can dance to big band music.

For dinner? It's impossible to tell you about all the great restaurants in San Francisco, but I recommend Lehr's Greenhouse, The Golden Dragon, New Pisa, La Mère Duquesne, or then Tadich Grill.

(Map labels: San Francisco Bay, N, Fisherman's Wharf, Beach Street, Lombard Street, North Beach, Columbus Avenue, Telegraph Hill, Hyde Street, Grant Avenue, Hyatt Regency Hotel, Jackson Street, Powell Street, Chinatown, Van Ness Avenue, California Street, Union Square, Post Street, Gerry Street, Market Street, ---- Cable car route)

Second Reading

Reread "A Day's Tour of San Francisco" and decide if each of the following statements is *True* or *False*. Then find the sentence in the reading or the illustrations that proves you are right. If the information is not given, write *NG*.

> Union Square is a good place for tourists to stay.
>
> *True*. One sentence says, "If you stay at a hotel near Union Square, you'll have lots of things to see just a short distance away." That's important for tourists.

1. San Francisco was built on flat land.
2. The "City by the Bay" is near an ocean.
3. Cable cars are recent inventions.
4. Cable cars must follow tracks, just like a train.
5. Many Chinese people live in San Francisco.
6. San Francisco is famous for its restaurants.
7. From the Hyatt Regency Hotel you can see the ocean.
8. You can dance at the Hyatt Regency any night of the week.
9. Telegraph Hill has an elevator for tourists who do not want to climb the hill.
10. The writer thinks that San Francisco is a good place to visit.

16 | Final Activity

Choose a vacation place that you know. Prepare answers to the questions below.

- How can you travel to this vacation place?
- What clothes should you take?
- What can you see and do there? (museums, art and musical events, historic buildings, scenery, ancient ruins, special celebrations, sporting events, etc.)
- What can you eat and drink there? Where can you do this? (local special foods, luxury restaurants, local drinks, etc.)
- Why is this a good place for a vacation?
- What can you buy there? (local crafts, inexpensive gifts, interesting clothing, etc.)

Now work with a partner. Ask and answer questions about each vacation place.

COMMUNICATION
Discussing travel plans ▪ Talking about plans and intentions

GRAMMAR
Verb + *to* + verb ▪ *To* + indirect object ▪ Indirect and direct objects

SKILLS
Reading and talking about a travel brochure ▪ Creating a travel brochure ▪ Planning an itinerary

Bon Voyage!

Gino and Cristina Leone are going to fly to Paris on their honeymoon. They bought round-trip tickets on TWA at the Wells Travel Agency. Their plane will leave New York on October 6 at 6:25 PM, and it will arrive in Paris at 7:45 the next morning.

Gino and Cristina will be in France for three days. They plan to see the Louvre Museum, the Eiffel Tower, and some of the other sights in Paris. Since they will be in Paris for only three days, they want to see as much as possible.

On October 9, they'll take an Alitalia flight from Paris to Rome. While in Rome, they'll spend a few days visiting famous sights, such as the Colosseum, the Forum, and the Vatican. Then, they'll take a train from Rome to Naples. Gino's parents and relatives live in Naples, and he and Cristina are going to stay there for a week. Cristina wants to make a good impression on her new in-laws. She's a little nervous about meeting her new relatives, but she's very excited about the trip.

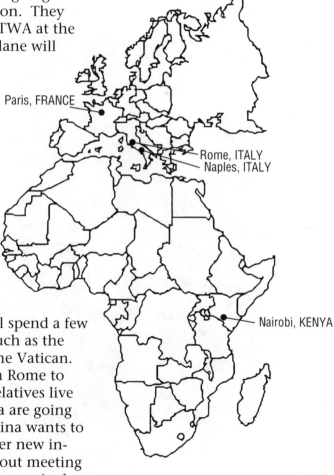

Paris, FRANCE

Rome, ITALY
Naples, ITALY

Nairobi, KENYA

Elinor Young also has travel plans. She has to attend a medical conference in Nairobi, Kenya. Her ticket cost $1,993. The fare was $1,990 and there was also a $3.00 tax. Elinor's not taking much luggage, because she doesn't need a lot of clothes. She's going to be very

busy at the conference, but if she has time, she'd like to visit a wildlife park. She's very interested in the protection of wild animals, such as elephants and rhinos. Elinor is very excited because this is her first trip to Africa. She's also a little bit nervous, because she doesn't like to fly.

SAVE AFRICAN WILDLIFE
Too many of these animals are killed!

african elephant

black rhino

These animals need *your* protection now!

Vocabulary in Context 🔲

Discussing travel plans

Complete the paragraphs with the correct words. Change the form of the word if necessary.

conference	luggage	rhino	tax
elephant	plans	round-trip	ticket
fare	protection	sights	wildlife park

   Elinor Young is going to a (1) _____ in Nairobi, Kenya. She bought a (2) _____ to fly from New York to Nairobi and back to New York. Her (3) _____ ticket cost $1,993. Elinor didn't want to take a lot of (4) _____ on her trip because she doesn't like to carry a lot of suitcases. She hopes to visit a (5) _____ in Kenya because she's interested in wild animals. (6) _____ and (7) _____ are wild animals that need (8) _____ .
   Cristina and Gino are excited about their honeymoon (9) _____ . The (10) _____ for their tickets is $2,200. They also have to pay a (11) _____ of $3.00 on each ticket. They plan to go sightseeing in Paris and Rome, and they also want to see the (12) _____ in Naples.

2 **Presentation** 🔲

Talking about plans and intentions

> To talk about plans and intentions, use the verbs below in this way:
>
> verb + **to** + another verb
>
> | **begin** | **forget** | **need** | **promise** | **start** |
> | **decide** | **hope** | **plan** | **remember** | **try** |

1. Elinor **plans to visit** a wildlife park in Kenya.
2. Gino and Cristina **decided to go** to France and Italy on their honeymoon.
3. Elinor **promised to send** postcards to her children.

3 Practice

**Make sentences using *to* and one of these verbs.
Some verbs can be used more than once.**

buy	go	pack	send	write
get	make	see	take	visit

> Gino and Cristina plan / to Paris and Naples on their honeymoon
>
> Gino and Cristina plan to go to Paris and Naples on their honeymoon.

1. they need / plane reservations
2. they decided / round-trip tickets to Paris
3. Cristina started / ready for the trip last week
4. she remembered / presents for Gino's family
5. she forgot / her bathing suit
6. she promised / postcards to all her friends
7. she'll try / a lot of postcards in Paris
8. Gino and Cristina hope / a lot of sights in Paris
9. they're beginning / excited about their trip
10. Cristina and Gino plan / Colosseum

4 Reentry

Talking about the future

A. **Work with a partner. Ask and answer questions about Gino and Cristina's trip using *will*.**

> go to England // France and Italy
> A: Will Gino and Cristina go to England?
> B: No, they won't. They'll go to France and Italy.

1. travel by boat // plane and train
2. be in France for a week // three days
3. go to Monaco // Paris
4. leave for Naples on September 11 // October 11

5. stay in Naples for a month // a week

6. stay in a hotel in Naples // Gino's family

B. **Now ask and answer questions about Elinor Young's trip using *will*.**

> Nigeria // Kenya
>
> A: Will Elinor go to Nigeria?
> B: No, she won't. She'll go to Kenya.

7. attend a wildlife protection conference // medical conference

8. visit a museum in Paris // wildlife park in Kenya

9. take much luggage // one suitcase

10. travel by train // plane

5 Reentry

Correcting information

Correct the sentences below using the information from the description of the characters' trips on pages 143-144.

> Gino and Cristina are going to stay at a hotel in Naples.
>
> No, they aren't. They're going to stay with Gino's family.

1. Elinor is going to Zaire.

2. She plans to attend a conference on African history.

3. Elinor hopes to visit a church in Kenya.

4. Gino and Cristina will leave New York on October 5.

5. Gino and Cristina are going to Venezuela for their honeymoon.

6. They're going to travel by boat from Rome to Naples.

7. Gino and Cristina will visit Cristina's family in Bogota.

8. Elinor will have to take a lot of clothes.

9. Elinor will attend a conference in Paris.

10. On October 9, Cristina and Gino will fly from Paris to Naples.

6 Interaction

Pretend you're leaving on a trip and you see a friend at the airport. Have a conversation with your friend about where you are going.

> A: Hello, _____ ! What are you doing here?
> B: I'm going to _____ on vacation. What about you?
> A: I'm going to | see | _____ .
> | visit |
> B: That's _____ . Oh, they're announcing my plane!
>   I have to go. Have a _____ trip!
> A: You, too. Give me a call when you get back.
> B: OK, I'll do that. We can get together and talk about our trips.

7 Reentry

Asking for information

Read the itinerary. Then work with a partner, and ask and answer ten questions about Fernando Sanchez's travel schedule.

ITINERARY FOR FERNANDO SANCHEZ			
Date	Flight	Departure and Arrival	Plans
November 12	American Airlines #907	Leave Miami: 6:20 AM Arrive Mexico City: 11:35 AM	attend a business meeting, go to museums, see ruins
November 18	Air Panama #501	Leave Mexico City: 2:45 PM Arrive Panama City: 7:00 PM	attend a reception
November 19	Lloyd Aereo Boliviano #100	Leave Panama City: 1:00 AM Arrive La Paz: 8:20 AM	visit friends, play tennis
November 21	Lan-Chile #494	Leave La Paz: 1:45 PM Arrive Santiago: 6:25 PM	attend a conference, attend a soccer game
November 27	American Airlines #1	Leave Santiago: 1:30 PM Arrive Buenos Aires: 4:14 PM	give an interview, attend meetings
December 2	Pan Am #202	Leave Buenos Aires: 5:30 PM Arrive Rio de Janeiro: 8:15 PM	go to beach, visit cousins
December 8	Pan Am #440	Leave Rio de Janeiro: 10:30 PM Arrive Miami: 5:50 PM	go home from airport by taxi

> A: When will Mr. Sanchez arrive in Mexico City?
> B: On November 12th at 11:35 AM.
> A: What airline will he fly on?
> B: American Airlines.
> A: What flight will he be on?
> B: Flight 907.
> A: What does he plan to do there?
> B: He plans to attend a business meeting, go to some museums, and see some ruins.

8 Listening

Number your paper from 1-10. Passengers are talking to a ticket agent at the airport. Listen to the passengers' questions and write the letter of the correct answer from the ticket agent.

1. a. No. You're too late for Flight 193.
   b. Yes, but there's another flight in an hour.
   c. Yes, but you must hurry to Gate 12 to make it.

2. a. Flight 201. It leaves at 9:15.
   b. Gate number 16 on the South Concourse.
   c. Two seats, one aisle and one window.

3. a. There and back.
   b. It's $549 round-trip.
   c. Three days round trip.

4. a. Dinner will be served.
   b. Gate sixteen.
   c. At 9:50 AM.

5. a. Yes. Walk straight ahead and you'll see it on the right.
   b. Yes. It's on the highway, about two kilometers from here.
   c. Yes, it's a restaurant.

6. a. Yes. The plane will depart on time.
   b. Yes, if you don't have any luggage.
   c. No, you have to buy your ticket two weeks in advance.

7. **a.** No, you'll have to buy your ticket in advance.
   b. You can stay there for two weeks only.
   c. Yes, but you will have to pay more.

8. **a.** It's spaghetti or chicken with vegetables.
   b. Children under the age of two don't have to pay.
   c. Yes, we have diapers and baby food.

9. **a.** Yes, you will get beverages and lunch.
   b. The flight attendants will serve you.
   c. Yes, you can get a good meal at the airport restaurant.

10. **a.** It's about 11,000 meters.
    b. The altitude is 33,000 feet.
    c. It's about 3 hours and 35 minutes.

9 Presentation

To + indirect object

> Use **to** before an indirect object with verbs such as:
> **send, give, sell, read, teach, show, write.**

1. Cristina will **send** a postcard **to** Sekila.
2. She will **give** a pearl necklace **to** her mother-in-law in Naples.

10 Practice

Make sentences using *will* and *to*.

> Cristina / write a letter / her mother
> Cristina will write a letter to her mother.

1. Liz / send her résumé / the airline
2. Gino / teach English / his brother
3. Cristina / show the wedding pictures / her sister-in-law
4. Gino's sister / teach Italian / Cristina
5. Cristina / read a story / her nephew
6. Tom / sell his old car / Mike
7. Elinor / give some African crafts / her family
8. Elinor / send postcards of African wildlife / her children

11 Presentation 📻

Indirect and direct objects

> Indirect objects can also come before the direct object. In this case, the preposition is eliminated.

1. | Elinor is going to give **some gifts** to **her children**.
   | Elinor is going to give **her children some gifts**.

2. | Gino is making **a pizza for Liz**.
   | Gino is making **Liz a pizza**.

> With **cost** and **ask**, you can make sentences in only one way.

1. The plane tickets cost **Cristina's parents $2,200**.
2. Tom asked **Cristina a lot of questions** about their honeymoon plans.

12 Practice

Make sentences placing the indirect object *before* the direct object.

> Cristina and Gino will send a postcard to Sekila.
>
> Cristina and Gino will send Sekila a postcard.

> I'm going to buy a sweater for my brother.
>
> I'm going to buy my brother a sweater.

1. Sam gave a gift to Toshio.
2. Cristina wrote a thank-you note to her aunt.
3. Cristina's going to send a letter to her uncle.
4. Tom's buying some books for his children.
5. Gino got a calculator for his sister.
6. Mike's making a big dinner for Bob.
7. Cristina will teach some English words to Gino's family.
8. The store sold some bad milk to Gino.
9. Elinor sent a postcard of an elephant to her family.
10. Carmen bought a beautiful sculpture for Cristina and Gino.

13 Practice

Work with a partner. Make past tense sentences two ways, if possible. One student will make a past tense sentence one way, and the other student will make a past tense sentence in a second way, if possible.

> Gino's mother / send / Cristina / a wedding gift
> A: Gino's mother sent Cristina a wedding gift.
> B: Gino's mother sent a wedding gift to Cristina.

1. Cristina's friends / give / Cristina / some beautiful wedding gifts
2. Cristina / ask / the ticket agent / a question
3. Elinor / show / her family / a brochure about Nairobi
4. the plane ticket / cost / Elinor / $1,993
5. Cristina / send / her mother-in-law / a thank-you note
6. Cristina's parents / write / Cristina / a letter
7. Gino / teach / Cristina / some Italian
8. Elinor / ask / a patient / some questions
9. Howard / give / Elinor / some aspirin
10. Cristina and Gino's honeymoon / cost / them / more than $3,000

14 Practice

Make sentences using pronouns as direct objects.

> Toshio's sister was in the hospital. // Toshio / send a card
> Toshio sent her a card.

1. Bob was sick last week. // The doctor / give some medicine
2. Sekila didn't call her parents. // She / write a letter
3. Lisa and Bob were hungry. // Adela / make lunch
4. I wanted some new clothes. // My sister / buy / a shirt
5. Toshio's birthday was last week. // The Logans / sent a card
6. Sam and Bob were at the Roma. // Gino / make spaghetti
7. Gino and Cristina were at the travel agency. // Tom / gave some brochures
8. Elinor likes elephants. // Howard / gave a small elephant sculpture
9. We were very thirsty. // Our friends / give some lemonade
10. I don't have time for a big meal. // Can you / make a sandwich

15 Reading

Before You Read

1. Have you ever read a travel brochure carefully? What kind of information do you look for?
2. What words or phrases in a travel brochure make you want to go to the place described?
3. What information in a travel brochure makes you decide *not* to go to the place?

Useful vocabulary:

1. **century:** 100 years
2. **citrus:** Oranges, lemons, limes, and grapefruit are *citrus* fruits.
3. **conch:**
4. **frequent:** very often
5. **guava:** a tropical fruit
6. **mainland:** the principal land of a country; not the country's islands
7. **palm:**

8. **seaport:** a place where large ships can go in and out; a port on an ocean or sea
9. **southernmost:** farthest to the south
10. **spiny lobster:**
11. **stone crab:**
12. **tart:** sharp or sour taste

First Reading

Read the questions below before reading the travel brochure. Think about the questions as you read. After reading, discuss your answers in small groups.

1. In what state is the city of Key West?
2. How old is the city of Key West?
3. What are the people in Key West like?
4. What kinds of trees can you find in Key West?
5. Where does the Overseas Highway start? Where does it end?
6. What do you think the Overseas Highway looks like? (Hint: Look at the map.)
7. Describe the summer weather in the Florida Keys.
8. What clothing should you wear in the Florida Keys in the summer?
9. What kinds of seafood can you eat there?
10. What kinds of fruit come from the Florida Keys?

Come to Key West

and Leave Your Worries Behind!

Key West first appeared on maps in the late 1700s. A century later, the island city had become the busiest seaport in Florida. Today, the colorful history of the nation's southernmost city can be seen in its historic houses, its charming palm-lined streets, and its independent people.

How to Get There

You can reach Key West by land, by air, or by sea. If you are driving, take the Key West exit from the Florida Turnpike. This will take you to the West Dade Tollway, which connects with U.S. 1 in Key Largo. This is where the famous Overseas Highway begins — it will take you all the way across the Keys until you reach Key West.

If you want to get to Key West by air, there are frequent flights from Miami International Airport and from many other Florida airports. If you want to go by sea, there are several ships that stop at Key West, or you can sail in your own boat — there are plenty of marinas in Key West.

Weather Conditions/What to Wear

The temperature in the Florida Keys ranges from the low 80s in July to about 70 degrees in winter. In summer the islands of the Florida Keys are cooler than mainland Florida because of the ocean breezes. These same winds make the Florida Keys warmer than the mainland in the winter.

Dress is casual. Bathing suits, shorts, and sandals are about all you need during the day. More formal clothes are appropriate for the evening.

What to Eat

You'll want to try the local delicacies from the land and the sea. There's conch, spiny lobster, shrimp, stone crabs, and many kinds of fish. There is tropical fruit with a flavor like nowhere else. There are very small oranges with a tart, sour taste, and guava and sea grapes. And of course, the famous Key Lime, a tiny citrus fruit that is an important ingredient in Key Lime pie and Key Lime cakes.

For more information contact:
FLORIDA KEYS & KEY WEST VISITORS BUREAU
P.O. Box 866 — Key West, FL 33041 * U.S. Toll Free 1-800-FLA-KEYS

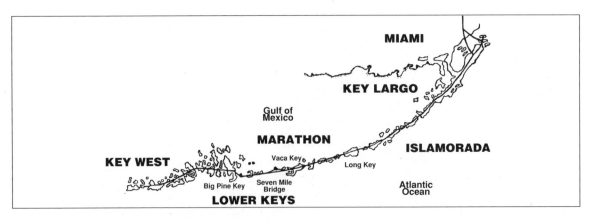

Second Reading

Read the travel brochure again and write ten questions about it. Exchange questions with a classmate and answer your classmate's questions. Then correct your classmate's answers to *your* questions! How many correct answers did you have? Which of your classmate's questions were difficult to answer?

16 Writing

Write a short travel brochure about the city or country where you live. Use colored pens, pictures from magazines, and anything else to make your brochure look real. Answer the following questions in your brochure:

- Why should someone visit there?
- What can you see?
- What can you do?
- What can you eat?
- What can you buy?
- What kind of weather will you have?
- What clothes should you take?
- How can you get there (plane, train, bus, etc.)?

17 Final Activity

Work with two or three classmates. Share the travel brochures you wrote in *16*. Use information from your brochures to develop a one-week itinerary for a visitor from another city or country. Tell the class about your group's itinerary for the visitor, and give reasons for each activity.

> Our visitor will visit the Art Museum on Day 1 because she is a famous sculptor from (*country*).

> Our visitor will eat lunch on Day 1 at the Laguna Restaurant because he loves seafood.

ITINERARY

Day 1 _____

_____

Day 2 _____

_____

Day 3 _____

_____

Day 4 _____

_____

Day 5 _____

_____

Day 6 _____

_____

Day 7 _____

_____

COMMUNICATION
Expressing an additional negative statement ▪
Talking about things that are about to happen
GRAMMAR
Either ▪ *About to* + verb ▪ Contrasting *a little*
and *a few* ▪ *Much, many*, and *a lot of*

SKILLS
Listening to a tape ▪ Discussing
problems with relatives ▪ Reading a
travel article

On the Way

Cristina and Gino are on the plane to Paris. They make friends with Pierre Amblard, a French man on the plane.

PIERRE AMBLARD:	Are you going to Paris on vacation?
CRISTINA:	Yes. Actually, we're on our honeymoon. We'll be in Paris for a few days, then we go on to Rome and Naples.
PIERRE AMBLARD:	Paris is a wonderful city — and a great place for a honeymoon. There are so many beautiful sights to see, so many wonderful things to do!
GINO:	Oh, we know. We plan to see the Louvre, the Eiffel Tower . . .
CRISTINA:	And Notre Dame . . .
PIERRE AMBLARD:	One night you should have dinner in the Latin Quarter. There are a lot of good, inexpensive restaurants there . . . and it's very romantic.
CRISTINA:	Oh, I think our hotel is near the Latin Quarter. We'll be sure to go there. Thanks for the suggestion.
PIERRE AMBLARD:	And you should also visit the Marais Quarter.
GINO:	Oh? We don't know about that.
PIERRE AMBLARD:	Well, it's very old and very interesting. You can see lots of historic buildings, the Pompidou Center, the Picasso Museum. You can eat in great restaurants and walk through charming streets. There's an article in this magazine about the Marais. You're welcome to take it with you.
CRISTINA:	Oh, thank you. It sounds fascinating.

FLIGHT ATTENDANT:	Ladies and gentlemen, we are about to land at Charles de Gaulle Airport. Please fasten your seat belts.
CRISTINA:	Oh! I can't wait to see Paris!
GINO:	I can't either. Oh, look, there's the Eiffel Tower!

1 Presentation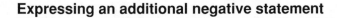

Expressing an additional negative statement

> Use **either** to express an additional negative statement.

1. Cristina **can't** wait to see Paris. Gino **can't either**.
2. Gino **isn't** from Venice, and he **isn't** from Rome **either**.

2 Practice

Make sentences with _either_.

> Gino doesn't work on Sunday. // Monday
> A: Gino doesn't work on Sunday.
> B: He doesn't work on Monday either.

1. Dr. Young won't be here today. // tomorrow
2. Gino wasn't nervous about the flight. // Cristina
3. Cristina can't ski. // skate
4. Gino and Cristina aren't traveling by boat. // Elinor
5. I can't get there by bus. // train
6. Pierre Amblard isn't an artist. // writer
7. My mother isn't very tall. // I
8. The Leones don't have a lot of money. // the Logans

3 Interaction

Work with a partner. Take turns agreeing with your partner's suggestion.

> A: I can't wait to _____ .
> B: I can't either. I really want to _____ .
> A: I do, too.

Presentation

Talking about things that are about to happen

About to means that something will happen *very soon*.

A

The plane is **about to** land.

B
Gino and Cristina are **about to** have breakfast.

C
The plane is **about to** take off.

5 **Practice**

Write two sentences about each picture using *about to.* Then sit with a group of three classmates. Compare your answers. How many different answers does your group have?

The Logans are about to go to the beach. They're about to leave.

1.

2.

3.

4.

5.

6.

6 Presentation 📼

Contrasting *a little* and *a few*

> **A little** is used with noncountable nouns. It means a small *amount*.
>
> **A few** is used with countable nouns. It means a small *number*, usually between two and five.

1. Cristina speaks **a little French**. She knows **a few words**.
2. Gino has only **a little money** in his pocket. He has only **a few dollars**.
3. They have **a little time** before their flight. They have **a few minutes**.

7 Practice

Make sentences using *a little* or *a few*.

> Gino and Cristina are taking only two suitcases. // luggage
> They're taking only a little luggage.

1. Cristina packed three dresses. // dresses
2. The Leones will stay in Paris for three days. // days
3. They have one day to visit museums. // time
4. They have a few hours to go sightseeing before they leave for Italy. // free time
5. Cristina learned a few Italian words before her trip. // Italian
6. She plans to buy two or three gifts in Naples. // gifts
7. Cristina wants to send some postcards to the United States. // postcards
8. Gino wants to buy a necklace and some earrings for Cristina. // jewelry
9. Pierre Amblard brought his children four books in English. // books in English
10. Elinor will be in Nairobi for four days. // days

8 Practice

Work with a partner. Take turns offering something to eat or drink and giving a polite response using *a little* or *a few*.

> milk
> A: Would you like some milk?
> B: Yes, please. I'd like a little.

1. grapes
2. salad
3. crackers
4. cheese
5. spaghetti

6. pepper
7. tea
8. french fries
9. coffee
10. tomato slices

9 Presentation

Much, many, and *a lot of*

---

1. Use **much** with noncountable nouns.

   Do you have **much luggage**?

   I don't have **much time** to spend with my family.

2. Use **many** with countable nouns.

   Do you have **many suitcases**?

   I don't have **many hours** to spend with my family.

3. **A lot of** is informal.
   Use **a lot of** with noncountable and countable nouns.

   Do you have **a lot of luggage**?

   Do you have **a lot of suitcases**?

4. **Much** is usually replaced by **a lot of** in affirmative statements.

   I have **a lot of luggage**.

---

10 Practice

Complete the sentences with *much, many*, or *a lot of*.

1. Do you have _____ money to spend in Paris?

2. The travel agent didn't give me _____ information.

3. Paris has _____ beautiful old buildings.

4. Pierre Amblard gave the Leones _____ good advice.

5. I don't have _____ French books to study.

6. Were there _____ people on the plane?

7. Cristina doesn't speak _____ Italian.

8. I'm usually nervous during a flight, so I don't eat _____ food.

9. Cristina and Gino won't have _____ time in Paris.

10. Elinor has _____ things to do before her trip.

11 Reading

Before You Read

1. Would you like to visit Paris? Why or why not?

2. What do you like to do most on a vacation?

3. Think of a city that you know well. What things would you recommend to a visitor to see and do there?

First Reading

You are going to read a travel article about the Marais Quarter in Paris. Pierre Amblard gave this article to Cristina and Gino. There are *many* new words in the article! You can understand the article better if you read it cooperatively. Follow these directions:

1. Sit in groups of four.

2. Read each paragraph silently, then discuss any difficult words or ideas.

3. Take turns being the discussion leader.

Petit Paris

The Marais offers the essence of the City of Light in one small quarter

by Mary Alice Kellogg

Paris for the business traveler can be as intimidating as it is beautiful. When free time is limited, the biggest mistake is to try to see all of this city at once. Consider, instead, a visit to one small, manageable *quartier*.

The Marais, located on the Right Bank between the Bastille and the Pompidou Center, has it all: a history as textured as any in Paris; more important architecture per square inch than any other neighborhood; and the most exciting museums, restaurants, and shops around.

A walk here takes you to some of the most charming and quiet streets in all Paris. Start at the place des Vosges, the heart of the Marais completed in 1612 and Paris's oldest square. No. 6 is the Victor Hugo Museum, filled with memorabilia of the author who lived there. The surrounding streets of the square, especially the rue des Francs Bourgeois, are lined with shops — some modern, others cluttered to the ceiling with antique silver, crystal, linens—a browser's dream.

If all this makes you hungry, you're in luck. Paris's newest three-star restaurant, Le Ambroise, is located on the place des Vosges. So is Coconnas, popular for lunch and dinner.

The blockbuster Picasso Museum on rue de Thorigny is a must — but not on weekends, if you can help it. For those who truly love Paris, the Hotel Carnavalet is devoted to the history and culture of the city.

Aside from its museums, restaurants, and cafés, the Marais is one of the loveliest places in Paris to walk. Stroll endlessly, through its maze of narrow and twisting streets. Around this corner a small café right out of the 18th century; across the street the studio of the newest fashion-design sensation; up the next block a shop selling 19th-century watercolors for a song. Just ask — The Marais will deliver.

Read the information about the Marais Quarter again. Then write *T* (True), *F* (False), or *NG* (Not Given) for each of the following statements.

1. The Marais Quarter is a small section of Paris.
2. All of the buildings in the Marais are modern.
3. It's necessary to take a taxi to go from one part of the Marais to another.
4. You can buy many beautiful things in the shops.
5. Victor Hugo died in this part of Paris.
6. There are excellent restaurants in the Marais.
7. The largest museum in Paris is in the Marais.
8. It's fun to take long walks around this part of Paris.
9. You should visit the Picasso Museum on a weekend.
10. The Hotel Carnavalet is a a very old building.

12 Listening

When Cristina met Gino's family in Naples she wanted to tell her sister Carmen all about it, but a telephone call from Naples to Bogota was too expensive. So Cristina decided to send Carmen a tape about her first day with her new in-laws.

First Listening

Number your paper from 1-38. Listen to the English version of Cristina's tape and write the missing words.

CRISTINA'S TAPE FOR CARMEN

October 11

Carmen, my honeymoon has been great until today. I finally met Gino's family this morning. Yes, you (1) _____ right. It's a *very* traditional family, and I (2) _____ living and working in the United States has (3) _____ me more independent — I like to do things (4) _____ think for myself!

Well, let me tell you the (5) _____ things first. The whole family came to the (6) _____ station to meet us — Gino's mother and father, (7) _____ sisters and brothers, his nieces and nephews, even his (8) _____ . They were all warm and affectionate at (9) _____ .

The grandmother is wonderful. She doesn't speak any (10) _____ , but I feel comfortable with her. I love (11) _____ watch her talking with Gino. I can't understand (12) _____ they say, but I understand a little when (13) _____ like Spanish. And when she (14) _____ at me and smiles, I know she likes me. I like her (15) _____ than anyone else in the family.

Gino's mother (16) _____ another story. I don't think she likes me. (17) _____ always looking at me with a cold stare. I (18) _____ my few words of Italian with her, (19) _____ she pretended not to understand, and Gino had to (20) _____ . Every time I say something and Gino translates it, she (21) _____ approve. She didn't like it when we were (22) _____ about our new apartment and I said that Gino will probably spend more time in the (23) _____ than I will. She asked me if we are (24) _____ to live in Italy, and she was positively icy (25) _____ I said we're going to stay in the (26) _____ . I felt so upset that I wanted to (27) _____ away by myself for a while, and I (28) _____ I wanted to take a walk alone. She (29) _____ hear of it. She said, "No, you must (30) _____ go out alone." She made me feel like she (31) _____ want me in the family.

My day (32) _____ in tears. I guess I'm just too (33) _____ for her. Gino has been very sympathetic, though. (34) _____ says not to worry, that it's (35) _____ a difference in cultures. Maybe he's right. Now that I've (36) _____ you all this I feel calmer and I (37) _____ that Gino's mother is very much like *our* (38) _____ in many ways! What do you think, Carmen? Please give me some good advice!

Second Listening

Number your paper from 1-6. Find each of the following expressions in the text for Cristina's tape. Then listen to Cristina's tape again, and guess the meanings of these expressions from the context. Write the letter of the correct answer.

1. *His mother is another story* means
   a. his mother is different.
   b. his mother likes to read.
   c. his mother told Cristina a long story.
2. *With a cold stare* indicates that
   a. Gino's mother felt cold.
   b. Gino's mother couldn't understand Cristina.
   c. Gino's mother was angry.
3. *She doesn't approve* means
   a. she doesn't know Cristina very well.
   b. she doesn't understand Cristina's Italian.
   c. she doesn't like what Cristina says.
4. *She was positively icy* means
   a. she was a little angry.
   b. she was very cold.
   c. she was very bored.
5. *Ended in tears* means
   a. Cristina was very unhappy.
   b. Cristina argued with her mother-in-law.
   c. Gino was not nice to Cristina.

6. *A difference in cultures* means
  a. a difference in ways of thinking and living.
  b. a difference between mothers- and daughters-in-law.
  c. a difference in age.

13 Writing

A. Read the text of Cristina's tape. Take notes on the positive things and the negative things that happened to Cristina on her first day in Naples. Then sit with a small group of classmates and compare your notes. Does everyone agree? Why or why not?

Positive Things	Negative Things
_____	_____
_____	_____
_____	_____
_____	_____
_____	_____
_____	_____

B. Choose one of the three topics below to write about.

a. Carmen's advice to Cristina
b. What Gino's mother wrote in her diary about her meeting with Cristina
c. Gino's letter to his friend in Winfield about Cristina's first day in Naples

Use your own ideas, the notes you made about positive and negative things that happened to Cristina, and information from the group discussion. Show your first draft to a classmate and ask for suggestions. Revise your draft to make it more interesting. Finally, work with a partner to check spelling and grammar.

14 Final Activity

Work in groups of four. Read the information about the travel contest. Write a group entry for the travel contest. Present your group entry to the rest of the class. The class will vote on the best group entry. Good luck!

> **TRAVEL CONTEST**
> *Win a free trip to Paris!*
>
> What would you like to see and do in the City of Light?
> Describe how you would spend 5 days in Paris.
> Write your description in 50 words or less.
>
> *The best entry will win 4 free tickets to Paris.*

UNIT 14

COMMUNICATION
Talking about plans ▪ Asking about possession ▪ Making comparisons ▪ Agreeing with a negative statement ▪ Talking about past events ▪ Making a choice ▪ Talking about shopping

GRAMMAR
Questions with *whose* ▪ Comparative adjectives

with *more than* and *less than* ▪ *Neither* ▪ Irregular past tense: *spend, cost, pay* ▪ Forming nouns from verb + *-tion* ▪ Questions with *which* ▪ Irregular past tense: *blow, cut, light, put, sing, teach*

SKILLS
Writing about a party ▪ Listening to a phone call ▪ Reading about endangered wildlife

Away from Home

Elinor meets a friend from medical school, Dr. Millie Carson, at the conference.

MILLIE: Elinor! I'm surprised to see you here!

ELINOR: Millie, this is a surprise! I didn't know you were coming to this conference. How wonderful! Whose lecture are you going to?

MILLIE: Dr. Hassan's.

ELINOR: Oh, so am I. We can sit together. . . . Why don't we go sightseeing while we're here? Do you have any plans for after the lecture?

MILLIE: No, I don't.

ELINOR: Would you like to go to the outdoor market? I saw some lovely necklaces for sale in the hotel gift shop, but they cost a lot. They say they're less expensive in the market.

MILLIE: Yes, I'd love to. And maybe we can take a tour of the city one day, too.

ELINOR: That would be nice. Let's see . . . I can't go tomorrow.

MILLIE: No, neither can I. How about Thursday?

ELINOR: That's fine.

MILLIE: I think there are tours at 2:00 and 4:00. Which one's good for you?

ELINOR: The one at four is better. Then I can attend Dr. Yuji's lecture at two.

MILLIE: OK. That's good for me, too. What are you doing on Friday?

ELINOR: I'm not sure yet. I'd like to visit a wildlife park over the weekend.

MILLIE: A wildlife park?

ELINOR: Yes. You can see animals like elephants, zebras, and rhinos in their natural surroundings. In the wildlife parks the animals are protected. It is against the law to kill them.

MILLIE: I'd love to see animals that are free — instead of in zoos.

ELINOR: Then why don't we go together to a wildlife park this weekend?

1 Vocabulary in Context

Talking about plans

Reread the conversation between Elinor and Millie. Then choose the correct words to complete this paragraph. Change the form of the words if necessary.

lecture	surprise
market	surprised
natural surroundings	tour
protected	zoo

Elinor had a good time at the conference. She attended several good (1) _____ and had time to do some sightseeing, too. One day she met an old friend from medical school, Millie Carson. Elinor was (2) _____ and happy to see her. They spent a lot of time together. One afternoon they went to the (3) _____ , and they also went on a (4) _____ of Nairobi. Seeing Millie was a nice (5) _____ . Elinor told Millie about African wildlife parks. People cannot kill animals in wildlife parks because the animals are (6) _____ . Millie doesn't like (7) _____ because the animals are not free. She'd like to see free animals in their (8) _____ .

2 Presentation

Asking about possession

> Use **whose** to ask about possession.

A
A: **Whose** ticket is this?
B: Elinor's.

B
A: **Whose** lecture did Elinor go to?
B: Dr. Hassan's.

3 Practice

Work with a partner. You are two doctors attending the International Conference on Public Health. Take turns asking and answering questions about whose lecture each of you is going to. If you are both going to the same lecture, agree to go together.

A: Whose lecture are you going to on Tuesday morning?
B: Dr. Hamilton's. Whose lecture are you going to?

A: Dr. Hassan's.
B: Well, I'll see you afterwards.

A: I'm going to Dr. Hamilton's, too.
B: Great! Let's go together.

INTERNATIONAL CONFERENCE ON PUBLIC HEALTH
NAIROBI, KENYA
Lecture Schedule

Tuesday, October 15

9:30	Dr. Walid Hassan	Lake Room
	Dr. Harris Hamilton	Palm Room
	Dr. Marian Doran	Sea View Room
11:00	Dr. Pietro Franco	Sea View Room
	Dr. Charlotte Rivera	Lake Room
	Dr. Kim Joon	Palm Room
2:30	Dr. Nancy Savitz	Palm Room
	Dr. Chee Chittagong	Lake Room
	Dr. Regina O'Neill	Sea View Room
4:30	Dr. Choo Hong	Sea View Room
	Dr. Paul Messina	Lake Room
	Dr. Sawaki Yuji	Palm Room

Wednesday, October 16

9:00	Dr. Dolores Barbosa	Palm Room
	Dr. Roberto de Palo	Lake Room
	Dr. David Chomsky	Sea View Room
10:30	Dr. Walid Hassan	Lake Room
	Dr. Nancy Savitz	Palm Room
	Dr. Sandra Greenberg	Sea View Room
2:00	Dr. Bikkar Prakash	Sea View Room
	Dr. Yukari Ogura	Palm Room
	Dr. Tsui Chen	Lake Room
4:00	Dr. Marian Doran	Palm Room
	Dr. Hector Mendoza	Lake Room
	Dr. Igor Tikunoff	Sea View Room

4 Presentation

Making comparisons

> To form the comparative of adjectives of two or more syllables, use **more/less** + adjective + **than**.
>
> | | | |
> |---|---|---|
> | nervous | **more nervous** | less nervous |
> | spectacular | **more spectacular** | less spectacular |
> | modern | **more modern** | less modern |
>
> EXCEPTION: For two-syllable adjectives ending in -y:
> **happy** ⟶ **happier**   BUT   **less happy**

A

The James Hotel isn't as spectacular as the President Hotel.

B

The President Hotel is **more spectacular than** the James Hotel. The James Hotel is **less spectacular than** the President Hotel.

5 Practice

Make sentences using *more . . . than* **or** *less . . . than*.

> A room at the James Hotel costs $65 a night. A room at the President Hotel costs $110 a night. // less expensive
>
> A room at the James Hotel is less expensive than a room at the President Hotel.

1. The first lecturer wasn't very exciting, but the second one was. // less exciting
2. The James Hotel isn't as modern as the President Hotel. // more modern
3. The earrings at the market are very unusual, but the bracelets aren't. // more unusual

4. There aren't many people at the hotel swimming pool. There are lots of people at the public swimming pool. // less crowded
5. Elinor is very excited about being in Nairobi, but Millie isn't. // more excited
6. Elinor thought Dr. Hassan's lecture was good, but she thought Dr. Hamilton's was boring. // less interesting
7. The necklaces at the hotel gift shop are very expensive, but the ones in the market aren't. // more expensive
8. Millie thought that Dr. Doran was boring, but she enjoyed Dr. Barbosa's lecture. // more interesting
9. The view from Elinor's room is of the ocean and the city. Millie just has a view of the hotel garden. // more spectacular
10. Millie is very tired, but Elinor isn't. // less tired

6 Presentation

Agreeing with a negative statement

Use **neither** to agree with a negative statement.

1.	Elinor can't go to the outdoor market tomorrow afternoon. Millie can't go to the outdoor market tomorrow afternoon.	Elinor can't go to the outdoor market tomorrow afternoon. **Neither can** Millie.
2.	Dr. Hassan doesn't speak much English. I don't speak much English.	Dr. Hassan doesn't speak much English. **Neither do I**.
3.	Dr. Hassan wasn't at Dr. de Palo's lecture. Elinor and Millie weren't at Dr. de Palo's lecture.	Dr. Hassan wasn't at Dr. de Palo's lecture. **Neither were** Elinor and Millie.
4.	Elinor won't be in Nairobi next week. Millie won't be in Nairobi next week.	Elinor won't be in Nairobi next week. **Neither will** Millie.

7 Practice

Work with a partner. Use the information in the chart to make a negative statement and another sentence with *neither*, as in 6. Add your own information to the chart if you wish.

> Elinor doesn't like old hotels.
> Neither does Millie.

Who	Verb	What
Elinor	don't/doesn't like	tropical fruits
Millie	isn't/aren't seeing	the weather in Nairobi
Dr. Hassan	didn't go	any souvenirs
Dr. Yuji	didn't buy	sightseeing in the old city
My uncle	don't/doesn't eat	any patients this week
My teacher	isn't/aren't interested in	old hotels
My friends and I	can't enjoy	beef or pork
Children	wasn't/weren't happy about	gifts for the family
I		flying at night
Elinor and Millie		prices in the hotel gift shop

8 Interaction

Work in small groups. Each person makes a statement about something he or she likes or dislikes. The other students agree or disagree.

A: I love soccer.

B: So do I.

C: I don't like it.

D: Neither do I.

9 Presentation

Talking about past events

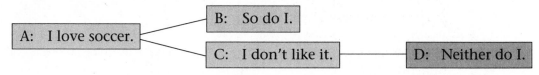

| spend $\longrightarrow$ **spent** | cost $\longrightarrow$ **cost** | pay $\longrightarrow$ **paid** |

1. Elinor **spent** a lot of money on her trip.
2. Her hotel room didn't **cost** much, but she **paid** a lot for food and transportation.

10 Practice

Complete the sentences with the past tense of *spend*, *cost*, or *pay*.

1. Elinor _____ a lot of money during her trip.
2. Her room _____ $320 for three nights.
3. She _____ for her hotel room on Friday morning.
4. Elinor's ticket _____ more than Millie's.
5. Millie _____ only $10 for a beautiful necklace.
6. Elinor and Millie _____ most of their money on gifts.
7. Gino and Cristina _____ as little money as possible.
8. However, their dinners in Paris _____ a lot.
9. Fortunately, Gino's parents _____ for their meals in Naples.
10. Cristina _____ about $45 on gifts for her family.

11 Presentation

Forming nouns from verb + *-tion*

Verb		Noun
describe	$\longrightarrow$	description
introduce	$\longrightarrow$	introduction
translate	$\longrightarrow$	translation
protect	$\longrightarrow$	protection

1. Elinor **described** the outdoor market. Her **description** was fascinating.

2. Elinor **introduced** Millie to Dr. Hassan. Millie was nervous before the **introduction** because Dr. Hassan is a very important person.

3. At the conference, someone had to **translate** Dr. Hassan's lecture from Arabic to English. Each time he spoke, someone gave the audience a **translation**.

4. Wildlife parks **protect** animals. **Protection** of some animals is important because there are not many of them.

12 Practice

Complete the paragraph with the words from *11*.

　　When he was in Naples, Gino saw his friend Tony. He (1) _____
Tony to Cristina. After the (2) _____ , they all went shopping. Cristina
was looking for a raincoat for her little nephew to (3) _____ him from
wet weather. She tried to (4) _____ it to the salesclerk, but her
(5) _____ wasn't very good because she didn't speak much Italian.
Gino and Tony tried to (6) _____ her English into Italian, but they
were laughing too hard and their (7) _____ wasn't very good. The
salesclerk thought they were looking for a raincoat for Gino, so she showed
them a large one. Cristina laughed and bought the large raincoat. "I guess
you need (8) _____ from wet weather, too," she said to Gino.

13 Presentation

Making a choice

Use **which** to ask a question about a choice among several specific things.

A
> A: **Which tour** does Elinor want to go on?
> B: The one at 4:00.

B
> A: Elinor and Millie can take a taxi or a bus to the market.
> B: **Which** is cheaper?
> A: The bus.

14 Practice

Work with a partner. Take turns asking and answering questions with *which*.

> guide / be more expensive // *The Guide to Luxury Travel*
> A: Which guide is more expensive?
> B: *The Guide to Luxury Travel.*

1. guide / contain information on inexpensive restaurants //
   The Student's Travel Guide
2. guide / give good histories of the different countries //
   The Guide to Luxury Travel
3. guide / have better maps // *The Guide to Luxury Travel*
4. hotel / be nearer the center of the city // the James Hotel
5. hotel / have a three-star restaurant // the President Hotel
6. hotel / Elinor want to stay in // the President Hotel
7. restaurant / serve better food // the Kilimanjaro Restaurant
8. restaurant / be noisier // the Pizzeria Napoli
9. restaurant / Elinor and Millie want to go to // the Kilimanjaro
   Restaurant
10. restaurant / more expensive // the Kilimanjaro Restaurant

15 Vocabulary in Context

Talking about shopping

1. Elinor looked at the bracelets **for sale** at the hotel gift shop.
2. The gift shop was having a big **sale** this week. The bracelets were
   cheaper than usual.
3. Last week the bracelets cost $50, but they're **on sale** this week.
   They only cost $35.
4. The salesperson at the gift shop **sold** Elinor a beautiful bracelet.

16 Practice

Match a sentence in the first column with a sentence in the second column. The first one is done for you.

> This scarf is inexpensive. It's on sale.

1. This scarf is inexpensive.
2. I'm tired of my old car.
3. I don't have a car now.
4. You can't buy this.
5. Let's go to Cindy's Boutique.
6. Look at this newspaper ad.
7. I like to shop in January.
8. My brother's friend bought 10 tickets for the concert.
9. Let's look at the jewelry.

a. They're having a big sale.
b. I sold it last week.
c. I'd like to sell it.
d. It's on sale.
e. It's not for sale.
f. All the stores have big sales.
g. He sold me two.
h. It's on sale this week.
i. There's a sale at Warner's.

17 Presentation

Irregular past tense: *blow, cut, light, put, sing, teach*

    While Gino and Cristina were in Naples, Cristina had a birthday. Gino's family gave her a birthday party. Gino's grandmother made a cake for her, and Gino **taught** his brothers and sisters to sing "Happy Birthday" in English and Spanish. After the birthday dinner, Gino **put** candles on the cake and **lit** them. Then everyone **sang** "Happy Birthday" — twice! Cristina made a wish, **blew** out the candles, and **cut** the cake. She **cut** the first piece for her mother-in-law, thanked her for the wonderful birthday party, and gave her a hug. Mrs. Leone's eyes **lit** up and she smiled at Cristina. "I'm glad you married my son," she said. Cristina was so happy that she wanted to cry. She **blew** her nose so that nobody would see her tears of happiness.

18 Practice

Work with a partner. Write three questions about Cristina's birthday party. Then sit with two other students. Ask and answer each other's questions.

19 Writing

Write about a birthday party or other party that you remember. Answer these questions:

• When was the party?
• Where was it?
• Who gave the party?
• Who was at the party?
• What did people do at the party?
• What did people eat at the party?
• Why do you remember this party?

When you are finished, share your writing with a classmate. Ask each other several follow-up questions.

20 Listening

Number your paper from 1-10. Elinor is calling home from Nairobi. Listen to her side of the conversation and answer the questions by writing *T* (true), *F* (false), or *NG* (not given).

1. Howard couldn't hear Elinor very well at first.

2. Elinor is having a terrible time in Nairobi.

3. Elinor told Howard about meeting Millie.

4. Elinor bought Howard and the kids gifts.

5. Elinor is arriving home at 8:25 on Tuesday.

6. Howard misses Elinor.

7. Millie bought some ivory earrings.

8. Elinor and Millie are going to a wildlife park.

9. Elinor hates elephants.

10. Elinor is afraid of the wildlife park.

21 Reading

Before You Read

1. What are your favorite wild animals?

2. Which countries do these wild animals come from?

3. Which wild animals are in danger?

> **Useful vocabulary:**
>
> 1. **at risk:** in danger
> 2. **brink:** edge
> 3. **conservation:** keeping wildlife safe
> 4. **decade:** 10 years
> 5. **endangered:** animals or plants that are almost all gone; very few are alive today
> 6. **extinction:** death of all the animals of a species
> 7. **habitat:** where animals and plants live
> 8. **species:** types of animals (elephants, rhinos, gorillas, pandas, jaguars, etc.)

First Reading

Think of the following statements as you read the article about World Wildlife Fund. When you finish reading, decide if the statements are True (*T*), False (*F*), or the information is Not Given (*NG*).

1. World Wildlife Fund protects wildlands and wildlife.

2. African elephants and Bengal tigers are not in danger.

3. WWF has a special program for wild horses.

4. Rhinos are very dangerous animals.

5. WWF helped to make almost 200 national parks.

6. WWF works only in Africa.

7. It is illegal to import ivory into the United States.

8. Jaguars are animals that live in Latin America.

9. Poachers try to kill wild animals.

10. People can give money to help WWF in its work.

World Wildlife Fund

Since its founding in 1961, World Wildlife Fund has protected hundreds of rare plant and animal species and millions of acres of wildlands through action projects on five continents.

Species Rescue

WWF helps stop the brutal killing of some of the world's most threatened animals, including Latin America's jaguar, the African elephant, the Asian snow leopard, and India's Bengal tiger.

Our Primate Action Fund brings a number of endangered species back from the brink of extinction. Our Panda Protection Program helps safeguard the few remaining pandas surviving in the wild. And WWF helps move a number of extremely rare black rhinos to remote areas of Zimbabwe and Kenya where they can be protected from poachers' bullets.

Habitat Protection

WWF helps create national parks and reserves around the world (almost 200!), including Masai Mara in Kenya, Annapurna Conservation Area in Nepal, and Manu National Park in Peru.

These projects are protecting millions of acres from overdevelopment and commercial exploitation, and making permanent places where endangered animals can live without danger.

Outreach and Intervention

WWF actively campaigns for major international agreements, legislation, and treaties on endangered species and habitats.

Our international trade-monitoring program, TRAFFIC, asks foreign governments to stop illegal trade in wild plants and animals. Our "Buyer Beware!" public awareness campaign helps travelers and consumers avoid illegal purchases of wildlife. And in response to a WWF request, President Bush banned the import of ivory into the U.S.

A Unique Opportunity

During the upcoming decade, World Wildlife Fund will continue to target action projects and training programs in critical areas where tropical forests and wildlife are most at risk. There is no time to lose.

Membership Contribution Form

☐ **YES!** I want to join World Wildlife Fund and help save wildlife and wildlands wherever and whenever they are threatened. Please put my membership contribution to work immediately to rescue endangered animals from extinction, defend the borders of national parks and reserves, curb illegal trade in rare species, train local park rangers, and help local peoples develop alternatives to destroying their natural heritage. I enclose a tax-deductible membership contribution of:

_____ $15 Member   _____ $250 Sponsor
_____ $25 Friend   _____ $500 Sustainer
_____ $50 Associate   _____ $1,000 Partner in Conservation*

* _____ Check here if you would like more information on the special benefits associated with Partners in Conservation.

Note: *A contribution of $15 or more entitles you to 12 months of membership benefits.*

Please fill in your name and address below:

__ Mr.   __ Mrs.   __ Ms.   __ Miss   __ Mr. & Mrs.

Name _____

Street _____

City _____ State _____ Zip _____

World Wildlife Fund
Dept. ZG11
1250 Twenty-Fourth Street, NW
Washington, DC 20037

Second Reading

Reread the brochure. Work with a classmate and answer the questions.

1. How old is World Wildlife Fund?
2. Give three examples of endangered animals.
3. How are endangered animals protected?
4. What does TRAFFIC do?
5. What is World Wildlife Fund going to do in the next ten years?
6. Name two things that WWF does with money from membership contributions.

Pretend you are shopping with a friend. Your friend sees a beautiful elephant sculpture in a shop window. It's made of ivory. He/She wants to buy it.

STUDENT 1: Try to convince your friend not to buy the ivory elephant.
Reasons you can give:
- To get ivory, people have to kill elephants.
- There are not many elephants left in Africa.
- We should protect elephants, not kill them.
  (Add more reasons.)

STUDENT 2: You want to buy the sculpture.
Reasons you can give:
- The sculpture is really beautiful.
- The elephant that this ivory came from is already dead.
- I can buy the sculpture and then give the same amount of money to World Wildlife Fund.
- There's nothing one person can do to protect elephants.
  (Add more reasons.)

After you and your partner have your discussion, talk about the reasons you each gave with the rest of the class.

VOCABULARY: Book 3

This vocabulary list contains the productive words as well most receptive words in Book 3. Productive words are those that students should know how to use. The unit number refers to when the word is first introduced productively. Receptive words are those that students need only understand. The unit number for these words is in parentheses.

(*n*) = noun; (*v*) = verb; (*adj*) = adjective; (*adv*) = adverb; (*pron*) = pronoun

A

a few   13
a little   13
a lot of   13
ability   (9)
about to   13
above   (1)
absent   (9)
absolute   (5)
abundant   (8)
accept   (8)
acceptable   (1)
according to   (7)
achieving   (8)
acquire   2
acquisition   (2)
acre   (14)
across   (4)
act   (8)
action   (1)
actively   (14)
activity   (2), 7
ad   (2)
add   (1)
additional   (8)
admission   (1)
adore   11
adverb   (5)
advice   (1)
aerobics   (7)
affect   (8)
affectionate   (13)
after   2
afterwards   (14)
against   (14)
age   1
agree   (1)
air   2
airfare   5
airline tickets   (10)
alive   (14)
all   (of)   7
allowed   (8)
almost   (1)
alone   (8)
aloud   (5)
already   (14)
although   (3)
altitude   (12)
always   5
ambulance   4
amount   (5)

ancient   11
angry   (5), 6
animal   5
anniversary   (1)
announce   1
announcement   1
annual   (1)
anonymous   (5)
antique   (2)
anxiously   (10)
any   8
anybody   (4), 9
anymore   (6)
anyone   (13)
anything   5
appear   (2)
appearance   (2)
appetite   (7)
application   (8)
appreciated   (4)
approve   (13)
area   (2)
arena   2
argument   (4)
around   1
arrival   1
arrive   1
as   (1)
as a/an ...   11
ashamed   (5)
aside   (13)
ask   12
asparagus   (8)
assistant   (6)
associate   (14)
astrologer   3
astrology   3
astronomer   (3)
astronomy   (3)
atmosphere   (11)
attack (*v*)   (5)
attend   (4), 14
author   (2)
authority   (5)
available   (2)
avoid   (14)
awareness   (14)
away   (1), 2

B

baby   (1)
back (*adv*)   (7), 9

background   (10)
bacon   (7)
bagel   (7)
baked   (8)
ballet   (11)
balloon   (2)
basis   2
bath   (2)
bathing suit   (11)
battle   (3)
bay   (11)
be born   1
be prepared   3
beading   (10)
became   2
because   6
become   3
begin/began   8, 12
beginning   (5)
behavior   (5)
behind   (5)
belief   5
believe   (3)
bell   (11)
below   (1)
benefit   (7)
best   (2)
best man   10
beverage   (8)
beware   (14)
billion   (3)
birth   1
blender   10
blew   14
blow   14
blow out   10
body   (5)
bon voyage   (12)
bonus   (8)
boring   (6)
boss   (5)
bottom   (1)
bought   10
bouquet   (10)
bowl   8
bowling   (7)
break down   10
breathing   2
bridal attendants   (10)
bride   1, 10
bridesmaid   10
bring   (1), 3
broccoli   (8)

brochure   (12)
broiled   (8)
bronchial   (2)
brought   (1)
brush   6
brutal   (14)
building   2
built   (11)
bulky   (7)
bullet train   11
bureau   (12)
burn   4
business   (3)

C

café   (11)
cafeteria   (7)
calculator   (6)
calendar   (3)
calorie   (7)
camera   (11)
campaign   (2)
candle   (10), 14
cards   1
carefully   (8)
careless   (6)
carpeted   (2)
carrot   (8)
carry   (5), 12
cartoon   (3)
cash   (5)
casserole dishes   10
cassette player   (5)
catch/caught   5
cause   (4)
cavities   6
ceiling   (13)
celebrate   1
celebration   1
celery   (8)
center   (3)
century   (2)
ceremony   (2)
certainly   (7)
champion   (1)
championship   (1)
change   (3)
character   (2)
charge (*v*)   (5)
charming   (12)
chart   (1)
chase   (11)

cheap   (8)
cheaper   14
check   3
checkup   6
cheer up   (9)
chef   (1), 5
chest   (9)
chief   5
childish   (5)
choice   (5)
choose   (1)
chores   1
civil   (1)
classified ad   (5)
clean   6
clear   11
clear up   2
climb   (4)
close to   2
cloud   4
clown   (2)
club   (8), 11
clue   (5)
collect   (2)
colorful   (10)
column   (1)
come back   6
come in   6
comfortable   (8)
comics   (5)
coming (*adj*)   (4)
comment   (5)
commit   (5)
committee   (4)
community   (4)
company   (1)
compare   (3)
comparison   (8)
compete   1
competition   1
complain   6
complete   (1)
condition   (7)
conference   12
connect   (12)
conservation   (14)
consider   (4)
consist of   (4)
consult   (7)
consume   (7)
consumer   (14)
contact   (4)
contain   (2)
contest   (13)
context   (5)
continent   (14)
contrast   (3)
contribution   (1)
control   4
convenience   2
conversation   (1), 5
convicted   (5)

convince   (6)
correct   (1)
correction   (5)
correspondent   (10)
cost   9, (past)   14
could   9
couldn't   9
counseling   (8)
counselor   (8)
county   (5)
couple   10
cover   (6)
crackers   (13)
craft   (11)
crash (*n, v*)   (4)
crazy   (5), 11
cream   8
create   (14)
crime   5
criminal   (5)
critical   (14)
crowded   (14)
cruel   (5)
cry   (4)
crystal glasses   10
cue   (4)
culture   (13)
cup   8
currently   (10)
customer   (3)
cut   (4), 14

D

daily   (8)
damage   (5)
damp   11
danger   (14)
dangerous   (5)
dark   (5)
deal with   (8)
death   (5)
decade   (14)
decide   1
decline   (1)
decrease   (7)
dedicated   (4)
deepen   (5)
defend   (14)
defending (*adj*)   (1)
delicacy   (12)
delicate   (10)
delightful   (11)
delivery   (2)
den   (2)
dental   (6)
dentist   6
depart   (10)
depend on   (6)
depressed   9
describe   (1), 14
description   (7), 14

desk clerk   (4)
dessert   (1)
destroy   (14)
detective   (5)
detergent   9
develop   (3)
devote   (5)
dial   (4)
diamond   (3)
diary   (8)
did   4
die   (4)
diet   (3), 7
difference   (3)
different   (1)
difficult   (1)
director   2
dirty   (5)
disagree   (1), 4
discomfort   (7)
discovered   (9)
discovery   (3)
disease   (9)
disgrace   (5)
dish   (1)
dislike   (14)
dispense   (1)
disprove   (3)
distance   (11)
divorce   1
do   4
donated   2
donation   (2)
door   (4)
downtown   2
drank   9
draw/drew   11
dream   (13)
drink   9
driver   (4)

E

each   1
earlier   (7)
earth   (3)
edge   (14)
editor   (5)
educated   (8)
effect   (7)
effective   (8)
either   (1), 13
election   (4)
electric   (10)
electricity   2
elegant   (10)
elephant   (2), 12
elevator   (11)
eligible   (4)
eliminate   (12)
elves   (2)
embarrassment   (1)

emergency   (4)
employ   (6)
empty   (5)
endangered   (14)
ending   (3)
endless   (11)
energy   (7)
engagement   1
enjoy   (2), 3
enormous   (3)
enough   (7)
ensure   (8)
enter   (4)
entertainment   (11)
entitle   (1)
entrée   (8)
entry   (13)
equal   (2)
era   (2)
escape   5
especially   (7)
essential   (2)
establish   (8)
even   8
ever   (8)
every   7
every other   7
everyone   14
exactly   (4)
examination   9
examine   (6), 9
except   (5)
exception   (8)
excessive   (5)
exchange   (2)
excitement   (10), 11
excuse   7
exercise   2
exhibit   2
exit   (12)
expand   (1)
expensive   (2), 5
explain   (2)
express   (13)
extensive   (2)
extinction   (14)
extra   2
extremely   (2)

F

fact   (7)
fair   (7)
fairly   (11)
fall (down)   11
family room   (2)
famous   (2)
far away   2
fare   (10), 12
farthest   (12)
fascinated   (3)
fat   7

less (7)
level (7)
license (10)
life 1
lift (7)
light (3), 14
likely 3
limbo (11)
lime (12)
limited (13)
lined (12)
linens (13)
liquids 9
list (2)
listed (adj) (7)
listing (2)
lit 14
liter (9)
living (n) (5)
loaf/loaves 5
lobby (4)
local (1)
located (13)
location 2
logical (3)
look at 6
look for 6
look up (7)
lose weight 7
lost 3, 8
loud 7
loudly 4
loveliest (13)
lovely (14)
low 5
lower (9)
luck (3)
lucky (3)
luggage 12
luxury 11

M

maid of honor 10
main (1)
maintained (2)
maintenance (8)
major (7)
management office (2)
manners (1)
many 13
map (11)
march (10)
mark (n) (5)
market 14
marriage 1
marry (3)
math (6)
meal 6
mean (v) 2
meaning (n) (1)
measure (8)

meatball (8)
medal 2
medical (5)
medicine 9
medium 7
meeting 4
member (4), 10
membership (4)
menu (8)
met 3
meter (12)
middle-aged (5)
might (6)
mind (5)
mine (1)
minor (7)
miss (4), 8
mistake 3
mix (5)
moderate (7)
modern (2), 14
modification (8)
moment (1), 4
money (1)
monitor (8)
more 1
more ... than 14
most 1
mother-in-law 1
motorcycle (2)
movement (3)
movie star (5)
much 13
mugger (5)
murder (5)
muscle (7)
musical (2)
My goodness! 9
mysterious (3)
mystery (5)
myth (7)

N

napkin 8
narrow (13)
native (10)
natural (8)
natural surroundings
  14
naturally (8)
necessarily (7)
necessary (4)
need 12
negative (13)
neighbor (4)
neighborhood 7
neither 14
nephew (14)
never 5
new 1
niece (10)

nightlife 11
nobody 14
noise 1
none of 7
normally (7)
note (1)
nothing 5
noun (3)
nowadays 1
nowhere (12)
numbered (3)
nutrition (8)

O

object (3)
observation (3)
observe (3)
obtain 10
occasion (10)
ocean (11)
of 2
off (7)
offer (2)
office 6
officer 5
official (5)
often 5
on a diet 7
on fire 4
on sale 14
on the premises 2
on time (7)
one-man (1)
one-on-one (2)
operate (1)
opinion (4)
opportunity 2
oral (1)
outdoor 14
outreach (14)
outside (2)
over (5)
over the years 2
overdevelopment (14)
overseas (12)
own (1)

P

pack (12)
page (1)
paid 3
pain (7)
pale (10)
pancake (7)
park (v) 3
part 2
part-time (3)
participate 1
past 2
patient 6

pay 1
peace (4)
pearl 12
pen pal (5)
per (2)
perfect (1)
perform (1), 2
performance (1)
period (7)
permanent (8)
personal (1)
perspire (7)
pet (2)
pharmacist 9
phase (8)
phone call (3), 10
photograph (n) (4)
photographer 4
physical (7)
pick out 10
pick up 10
picture 4
pie (12)
piece (3), 8
pills 9
pilot (5)
place (v) (12)
plan (1), 12
planet (3)
plans 12
plant (v) (3)
plate 8
play (n) (2)
pleased (1)
pleasure (2)
plus (2)
pocket 13
point of view (1)
point out (4)
police officer 4
polite (6)
politely (1)
popular (13)
pork (14)
position 3
positive (8)
possession (14)
possibility (9)
potluck (1)
predict 3
premature (7)
preparation (8)
prepare 4
prescribe 9
prescription 9
president (1)
pretend (1)
pretty (adj) 8
prevent (6)
previous (8)
primate (14)
prince (5)

principal (12)
principle (8)
print (5)
prison (5)
prisoner (5)
private 2
probably (1), 3
processed (8)
professional (8)
programming 1
progress (8)
promise (4), 12
promotion (3)
pronoun (3)
protect (5), 14
protected (adj) 14
protection 12
prove (11)
provide (8)
public (1), 2
pull 6
purchase (14)
put 14
put in (4)
put out 10
puzzled (1)

Q

qualification (4)
quantity (8)
quart 8
quarter past 2
quickest (7)
quiet (9)
quite (3)

R

raincoat (14)
raise (7)
ran (4)
rang 11
range (v) (12)
rapidly (7)
rare (14)
rarely 5
rather (8)
reach (4)
read (past) 3
read 12
ready (2)
real (1), 11
really (1), 3
reason 1
reasonable 2
receive 1
recent (9)
reception 1, 10
recommend (13)
record (6)
recreate (1)

reduce (7)
refer to (3)
refined (8)
reform (5)
refrigerator 3
refuse (1)
regular 2
regularly 7
relative (n) (5)
relatively (7)
release (5)
remain (8)
remember (1), 6
remote (14)
remove (9)
rent (2)
replaced (8)
reporter (1), 4
request (14)
require (7)
rescue 4
reservation (10)
reserve (n) (14)
reside (10)
resident (11)
resources (4)
respected (6)
response 2
responsible (8)
rest (2)
restful (7)
result (1)
resume (12)
retire 1
retired 1
retirement 1
return (1)
reverse (3)
review (n) (3)
revise (5)
revolve (3)
rewrite (4)
rhino 12
rich (1)
rights (1)
ring 11
risk (7)
robbed 5
robber (4), 5
robbery (4)
role (3)
romantic 11
roof 5
rose (10)
round-trip (10), 12
route (11)
rude (1)
rudeness (1)
ruins 11
rule (8)
ruler (3)
runway (4)

S

safe (5)
safety (5)
said (1)
sail (12)
sale (2), 14
salesperson 14
salt and pepper shakers 8
same (1)
sandy 11
sang (10), 14
sat down 11
saucer 8
save (1)
scale (8)
scan (2)
scarf/scarves 5
scene (4)
scenery (11)
schedule (8)
scholarship (1)
scientific (3)
score 1
scrambled (3)
scratch (5)
sculptor (12)
sculpture 2
sea 11
search (3)
section (3)
sedentary (7)
seem (7)
selection (4)
sell (8), 12
senator 4
send 1
senior (1)
separable (10)
separate (adj) (3)
separate (v) (6)
series (2)
serious 4
serve (8)
serving dishes 10
session (8)
set up (8)
setting (2)
several 1
shape 7
sharp (12)
sheets 10
ship (12)
shop (v) (3)
short of (1)
shot (5)
show (n) (1), (v) (3), 12
shower (4)
side (10)
side order (8)

sights (10), 12
sightseeing 12
sign 3
silently (10)
silverware 8
similarity (3)
simple (1), 4
since (1)
sing 14
sister-in-law (12)
sit (down) 6
situation (1)
skim milk (8)
skin (8)
sky 3
sleep/slept 8
slice 8
slow down (7)
smart (3)
smile (1), 11
smoke 4
snow (5)
so 1
so-called (5)
society (5)
soft-boiled (8)
sold 3, 14
solution (1)
solve (5)
some 8
some of 7
somebody 4
someday (3)
someone (3)
something 5
sometimes 5
song (2)
sore (7)
sound (9)
soup spoon 8
sour (12)
spare time (4)
speaker (6)
species (14)
specific (2), 4
spectacular 2
spend (6), 14
spent (8), 14
spoon 8
squad (4)
square (2)
stadium (1)
staff 2
stage (8)
stamp (2)
star 3
starch (8)
stare (13)
start (1), 4
start over (7)
state (1)
statue (11)

stay   (3)
steak   8
steal   5
steps   4
stole   5
stood   (4)
storm   (5)
straight   (1)
stranger   (3)
strength   (7)
stress   (8)
stroll   (13)
strong   (4)
studio   2
study (n)   (7)
stuff   (2)
substance   (9)
success   (8)
such   (1)
suggest   (5)
suggestion   (3)
summary   (2)
sun   (3)
sunset   11
support   (4)
surprise   3
surprised   14
surround   (5)
surviving   (14)
sympathetic   (13)
symptom   (9)
syrup   (7)

T

table   (3)
tablecloth   10
tablespoon   8
take care of   6
take it easy   (9)
take off   10
take turns   (1)
talented   (1)
tape   (13)
target   (14)
tasteless   (1)
taught   (8), 14
tax   (4), 12
teach   14
tear   11
teaspoon   8
techniques   (8)
teeth   6
telescope   (3)
television set   (5)
tell   1
tell time   (2)
teller   (11)

temperature   9
temple   11
test   (3)
than   (9)
than any other   11
there was   4
there were   4
thermometer   9
thief/thieves   5
thin   (6), 9
thing   1
thought   3
throw   4
throw away   (5), 10
ticket   12
tiger   (14)
tiny   (12)
tip   (5)
title   (1)
to   2
toast   8
toaster   10
together   (3)
told   9
took   (1), 5
toothache   6
toothbrush   (9)
top   5
topic   (11)
tore   11
tossed salad   (8)
tour   (11), 14
tournament   (1)
towels   10
town   (1), 2
toy   (2), 11
track   (11)
traffic   4
train (v)   (6)
training   (4)
translate   (13), 14
translation   14
transportation   (11)
treasure   2
trip   3
trophy   (1)
tropical   11
trouble   (5)
true   (2), 3
truly   (1)
try   1
tuna   (8)
turkey   (8)
turn (n)   (6)
turn off   10
turn on   (4), 10
tuxedo   10
twin   (2)

typical   (10)

U

ugly   (8)
ulcer   (9)
ultimate   (8)
ultramodern   2
unanswered   (5)
unbeatable   2
under control   (4)
unfair   (5)
unhappy   1
unique   (14)
unit   (2)
universe   (3)
unknown   (4)
unlock   (4)
unnecessary   (7)
until   (8)
unusual   2
upon   (3)
upper   (4)
used to   2
useful   (5)
usual   14
usually   5
utilities   2

V

vacant   (5)
value   (2)
van   4
variety   (8)
vase   10
veil   10
victory   (1)
view   (2)
vigorous   (7)
violent   (5), 7
visible   (5)
visit   (2), 12
visitor   (12)
vital   (8)
volunteer   (4)
vote   (13)

W

waiting room   (7)
walk-in closets   (2)
wall   4
way   (1)
wed   1
wedding   1
wedding party   10
weekly   (8)

weigh   7
weight   7
well-known   (1)
wet   (10)
when   4
whenever   (14)
wherever   (14)
whether   (1)
which   14
while   (3), 4
whisper   (10)
whole   (1)
whole-wheat   (8)
wholesome   (8)
whom   (2)
whose   14
why   1
wild   (1), 5
will   (1), 7
win   1
window   4 .
wise   (8)
within   (2)
without   (5)
witness   (4)
wives   5
woke up   3
wolf/wolves   5
women   5
won't   3
wonderful   (2), 11
wore   10
worker   4
world   2
world-famous   (11)
worry   (12)
wound   (5)
wrapped   (2)
write   11
write down   (6)
wrong   (1)
wrote   (5), 9, 11

Y

year   1
yell   4
yet   (14)
young   (5)
yourself   4

Z

zebra   (14)
zoo   14